batik
75 selected masterpieces

Rudolf G. Smend Collection

Contributors

Isa Fleischmann-Heck

Maria Wronska-Friend

Donald J. Harper

Rudolf G. Smend

Historical Photos

Hans van der Kamp

D1737313

Galerie Smend

Published by Tuttle Publishing,
an imprint of Periplus Editions (HK) Ltd.,
with editorial offices at 364 Innovation Drive,
North Clarendon, VT 05759 and 130 Joo Seng Road,
#06-01 Singapore 368357

ISBN 10: 0-8048-3895-X
ISBN 13: 978-0-8048-3895-5

Copyright © Galerie Smend 2006

Verlag / Publisher:
Galerie Smend, Köln
Mainzer Strasse 31,
50678 Köln, Germany
Tel.: +49 (0) 221 / 31 20 47
Fax: +49 (0) 221 / 93 20 7 18
E-mail: smend@smend.de
www.smend.de
© 2006 Verlag der Galerie Smend, Köln
Printed in Germany

Distributors:

Indonesia
PT Java Books Indonesia,
Kawasan Industri Pulogadung,
Jl. Rawa Gelam IV No. 9, Jakarta 13930.
Tel: (021) 4682 1088
Fax: (021) 461 0207
E-mail: cs@javabooks.co.id

Asia Pacific
Berkeley Books Pte Ltd, 130 Joo Seng Road
#06-01, Singapore 368357.
Tel: +65 6280 1330
Fax: +65 6280 6290
E-mail: inquiries@periplus.com.sg
www.periplus.com

North America, Latin America
Tuttle Publishing, 364 Innovation Drive,
North Clarendon, VT 05759-9436
Tel: +01 (802) 773 8930
Fax: +01 (802) 773 6993
E-mail: info@tuttlepublishing.com
www.tuttlepublishing.com

Front jacket:
Detail No. 39, S./p. 100/101
Photo: Royal or aristocratic bride,
Central Java, 1900-1910
photographer unknown
Collection Leo Haks, Amsterdam

Back jacket:
Photo Collage, walldecoration, c. 1900
Collection Hans van der Kamp, Den Haag

This page:
Detail No. 44, S./p. 107

Inhalt / Contents

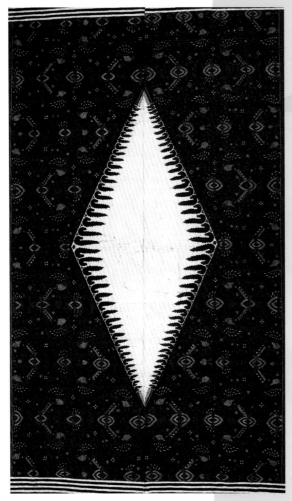

Dodot. Yogyakarta, c. 1930, 330 x 210 cm

Vorwort

Brigitte Tietzel

Es gibt sehr unterschiedliche Sammlertypen, wie es natürlich unterschiedliche Gründe dafür gibt, seine Sammelleidenschaft auf ein bestimmtes Gebiet zu richten: Glas beispielsweise oder Elefanten oder alte Rheinansichten.

Beneidenswert, wenn jemand, wie Rudolf Smend, als junger Mensch in die Welt zieht, auf der Suche nach etwas Besonderem, nach dem Sinn des Lebens, nach sich selbst – mit weniger möchte man sich nicht zufrieden geben – und es dann tatsächlich findet: auf dem Weg, der eigentlich ganz woanders hinführen sollte und aus Zufall. So jedenfalls beschreibt Rudolf Smend die Anfänge, eine Reise, die er mit 31 Jahren unternahm, die ihn nach Australien führen sollte und die vorzeitig in Indonesien, auf Java und Bali, endete. Dort wurde er zum ersten Mal mit gebatikten Bildern und Textilien konfrontiert, erlernte selber die Technik unter kundiger Anleitung und war von diesem fremden Land, seinen angenehmen, heiteren, liebenswürdigen Menschen, von der Schönheit der Landschaft ebenso wie von dem Reiz der völlig anderen Kultur so bewegt, dass es ihn für sein Leben prägte.

Die Reise in diese unbekannte Welt hat Rudolf Smends Leben verändert, das er, nach Köln zurückgekehrt, fortan, zum Teil wenigstens, Indonesien widmete. So ist diese Sammlung javanischer Batiken nicht nur ein Anhäufen von Textilien zu einem bestimmten Thema, sondern sie ist Ausdruck einer tiefen Liebe zu dem Land, das er seit jenem ersten Mal noch unzählige weitere Male besuchte. Und sie ist Ausdruck einer großen Freude über die vielen schönen Objekte, die, wie alle Textilien, geeignet sind, eine sehr unmittelbare Verbindung zu den Menschen, die sie einmal getragen haben, herzustellen. Ein schöneres Motiv zu sammeln, als solche Liebe und Nähe kann ich mir nicht vorstellen.

Wir freuen uns deshalb, die Sammlung von Rudolf Smend, der dem Museum durch eine Freundschaft mit dem ehemaligen Direktor Carl-Wolfgang Schümann und seit dem Einzug der Sammlung in die schönen Räume in Linn eng verbunden ist, heute im Deutschen Textilmuseum zeigen zu können. Dass dies gerade zum jetzigen Zeitpunkt geschieht, hängt mit einem „Jubiläum" zusammen, über das die Kuratorin der Ausstellung, Frau Dr. Isa Fleischmann-Heck, in diesem Buch gesondert berichtet:

Vor einhundert Jahren, 1906, eröffnete Friedrich Deneken, der umtriebige erste Direktor des Krefelder Kaiser Wilhelm Museums, die erste große Ausstellung indonesischer Kunstwerke in Krefeld und Deutschland überhaupt, die eine bedeutende Rolle für die Rezeption insbesondere der Batiktechnik spielen sollte.

Ich möchte Herrn Smend dafür danken, dass er seine Sammlung dem Deutschen Textilmuseum für diese Ausstellung zur Verfügung stellt und auch für die vielfältige Unterstützung, die er in all den Jahren dem Museum angedeihen ließ: Manchmal durch finanzielle Mittel, immer aber durch seine große Wertschätzung unserer Arbeit, die er nicht müde wurde, allen, mit denen er zu tun hat, zur Kenntnis zu geben. Er hat durch seine Anregungen und seine Mundpropaganda dem Museum über viele Jahre große Dienste erwiesen.

Wie ungewöhnlich er als Sammler ist, zeigt die Tatsache, dass das Hauptstück der jetzigen Ausstellung gar nicht sein eigenes ist, sondern dass er es an das Museum vermittelt hat (No. 39). Es handelt sich hierbei um eine ganz außergewöhnlich qualitätvolle Batik – Prada mit Tambal (Patchwork)-Motiven – die mit Gold belegt wurde und von der Nordküste Javas, aus Cirebon oder Semarang stammt. Sie wurde zu einem sehr frühen Zeitpunkt, nämlich bereits in den 70er Jahren des 19. Jahrhunderts, von einem niederländischen Verwaltungsbeamten, W.O. Gallois, gesammelt und muss kurz vorher, um 1860 - 1870, entstanden sein. Gallois, der seinen Dienst 1871 zunächst in eher untergeordneter Stellung im Generalsekretariat von Batavia aufgenommen hatte, beendete seine Karriere als Vizepräsident des „Council of the Indies" und unterstand dann direkt dem Generalgouverneur. Gallois' Sammeltätigkeit war bereits nach wenig mehr als zehn Jahren so erfolgreich, dass er 1883 Teile seiner Batiksammlung einer großen „Kolonial-Ausstellung" in Amsterdam zur Verfügung stellen konnte. Nach seiner Pensionierung kehrte er 1898 in die Niederlande, nach Den Haag, zurück, wo er 1917 starb. Die prachtvolle Batik, die jetzt durch

Vermittlung von Rudolf Smend vom Deutschen Textilmuseum angekauft werden konnte, stammt aus dem Nachlass der Enkelin, Annie Gallois, die 1984 starb.

Sri Sultan Hamengku Buwono X. Yogyakarta 1979
Jugendbild von 1979, Sultan seit 1988
Foto as a young man, he became sultan in 1988

Auch hier war die „Liebe" stärker als das „Besitzenwollen". Smend befand, dass ein solches Stück ins Museum gehört. Recht hat er. Die Verantwortung in der Sache übertrifft die Selbstsucht, die jeder Leidenschaft, vor allem der des Sammlers, eigen ist. Das macht die Zusammenarbeit mit Rudolf Smend so angenehm.

Dem Besucher wird sich die außergewöhnliche Schönheit des Stücks unmittelbar erschließen, dessen „patchwork" so vielgestaltig aus Quadraten, Rechtecken, diagonalen Balken gebildet wird, die doch zu einer wunderbaren Regelmäßigkeit und Ganzheit zusammengefügt sind. Der Glanz des Goldes spart nur jenen oberen Rand des Gewandes aus, der, um den Körper geschlungen, unsichtbar bleibt. Er spricht von Fürstenhöfen und Künstlern, die das Alltägliche weit hinter sich lassen. Er verlockt uns, einzutauchen in eine Märchenwelt.

Preface

Brigitte Tietzel

There are many different types of collectors, just as there are, of course, many different reasons why someone would focus their collecting passion on a specific field: for instance, glass or elephants or old views of the Rhine.

We envy people like Rudolf Smend who go out into the world when they are young in search of something special, to discover the meaning of life, to discover themselves – they would not settle for less – and then actually find it, quite by chance while travelling a path intended to take them elsewhere. This at least is how Rudolf Smend describes his beginnings – a journey he undertook at the age of 31 that was supposed to lead him to Australia and that ended prematurely in Indonesia, in Java and Bali. This was where he first encountered batik pictures and textiles, where he learnt the technique himself under expert guidance, and where this foreign country, its pleasant, serene and amiable people, the beauty of its landscape and the attraction of a wholly different culture moved him so much that it left its mark on him for life.

His journey into this unknown world changed Rudolf Smend's life, and he devoted at least part of it to Indonesia upon his return to Cologne. Thus this collection of Javanese batiks is not only an accumulation of textiles pertaining to a specific theme, but also an expression of deep love for a country that he visited countless times after that first visit. Moreover it is an expression of great joy about these many beautiful objects, which like all textiles are apt to evoke an immediate connection to the people who once wore them. I cannot imagine a finer motivation for collecting than such love and intimacy.

Rudolf Smend has had close links to our museum since the collection moved to its beautiful premises in Linn, and also due to his friendship with the former director, Carl-Wolfgang Schümann. Thus we

Workman of the Royal Dutch East Indies Army
Artillery and Munitions Factory at Bandung.
Slamat Djalan – Gute Reise/Good Journey.
Bandung, c. 1930

are very happy to have this opportunity of presenting his collection at the Deutsches Textilmuseum. The event takes place at this particular time because of an "anniversary" on which the exhibition curator, Dr Isa Fleischmann-Heck, will report elsewhere in this book: one hundred years ago, in 1906, Friedrich Deneken, the keen first director of the Krefeld Kaiser Wilhelm Museum, opened the first major exhibition of Indonesian artworks ever to be shown in Krefeld or Germany, and this show was to play a major part in the public response to this art, especially the batik technique.

I would like to thank Mr Smend for making his collection available to the Deutsches Textilmuseum for this exhibition, and for the many ways in which he has supported the museum over the years, sometimes in financial terms, but always through his great appreciation of our work which he never tired of promoting to everyone with whom he had dealings. His ideas and his word of mouth have been of great service to the museum for many years.

His unusual attitude as a collector is shown by the fact that the main piece of the current exhibition is not even his own; instead, he arranged for the museum to purchase it (No. 39). It is an unusually high-quality batik – a prada with tambal (patchwork) designs – covered in gold and produced on the north coast of Java, in the towns of Cirebon or Semarang. It was collected at a very early stage, in the 1870s, by a Dutch administration official, W.O. Gallois, and was probably made just before, in c. 1860 - 1870. Gallois initially began his service in 1871 as a rather lowly employee in the General Secretariat of Batavia and ended his career as the Vice President of the "Council of the Indies", in which position he was directly answerable to the governor-general. Gallois' collecting efforts were so successful that after little more than ten years he was able to make parts of his collection available for a major "Colonial exhibition" held in Amsterdam in 1883. Upon his retirement in 1898 he returned to the Netherlands, to The Hague, where he died in 1917. The splendid batik whose acquisition by the Deutsches Textilmuseum Rudolf Smend recently arranged, came from the estate of his granddaughter, Annie Gallois who died in 1984.

Here too, "love" was stronger than the "wish to own". Smend felt that a piece of this quality belonged in a museum. He was right. This sense of responsibility for one's cause overrides the selfishness inherent in every passion, especially a passion for collecting. That is what makes working with Rudolf Smend such a pleasure.

Visitors will immediately appreciate the extraordinary beauty of the piece whose "patchwork" is made up of such varied shapes – squares, rectangles and diagonal bars – that nevertheless combine into a whole of wonderful regularity and unity. The brilliant gold is applied everywhere except at the top edge of the garment that is invisible when wrapped around the body. It tells of princes' courts and artists who leave everyday life far behind. It tempts us to immerse ourselves in a fairytale world.

Card players. Batavia, c. 1885

EXOTISCHER HAUCH ÜBER KREFELD

Die Niederländisch-Indische Kunstausstellung 1906 in Krefeld und die deutsche Batik bis 1920

Isa Fleischmann-Heck

Blick in die „Niederländisch-Indische Kunstausstellung" im Krefelder Kaiser Wilhelm Museum 1906

The 1906 "Dutch East Indian Art Exhibition" at the Kaiser Wilhelm Museum Krefeld

Im April-Heft der Zeitschrift „Textile Kunst und Industrie" aus dem Jahr 1920 richtet ein nicht näher zu identifizierender Autor mit den Initialen H.B. einen verzweifelten Aufruf an die deutsche „Batik-Gemeinde": Einer „Verelendung der Batikkunst" sollte durch „künstlerische Einflüsse" entgegen gesteuert werden.[1] Einige Zeilen vorher beschreibt der Verfasser die Ursachen für das von ihm bezeichnete Übel genauer:

„Batiken finden heute nicht nur das Interesse des großen Publikums, für das diese wiedererstandene Technik beinahe geschmacksverheerend mit allen ihren verschiedenen brauchbaren und unmöglichen Anwendungen geworden ist, sondern auch [...] das des Fabrikanten. [...] Gehörte es früher zum guten Ton, daß ein junges Mädchen ‚brandmalte', so muß jetzt um jeden Preis gebatikt werden. Es gibt einfach kein Mittel, diesem Übel zu steuern [...]." Immerhin sei es im Wesentlichen Künstlern zu verdanken, dass „diese feine, in der rechten Hand erfinderischen Geistes geradezu überraschend wandelbare Technik nicht völlig in die Fänge nur dilettantischer geschäftüchtiger Leute gelangen konnte". Deshalb richtet sich der Appell des Autors schließlich vor allem an jene Künstler, die sich dem lockenden Ruf der Fabrikanten zu entziehen vermochten.[2]

Dieser erregte Kommentar eines kritischen Beobachters war nicht die einzige Äußerung, die Enttäuschung verrät über gewisse „Fehlentwicklungen" seit Einführung der Batiktechnik in Deutschland um 1900. Denn zwei Jahre zuvor, im März-Heft 1918 derselben Zeitschrift, schrieb bereits ein äußerst empörter J.A. Loebèr Jun., Professor der Kunstgewerbeschule in Elberfeld, Batik-Experte und Künstler aus den Niederlanden, einen zweiseitigen Artikel, knapp übertitelt mit „Batik". In diesem formuliert er sein Entsetzen über die gewissenlose Aneignung des Begriffs Batik von Seiten der Industrie für Seidenstoffe, die in Tritik- bzw. Plangi-Technik verziert werden.[3] „Speziell für die deutsche Gründlichkeit" sei dieser Name – Batik – sehr „beschämend"; resigniert stellt der Autor fest: „Für den Handel ist das Wort ‚Batik' nun einmal das Schlagwort geworden und aus Erfahrung weiß man genügend, daß sich so was nicht verdrängen läßt. [...] Es wäre deshalb sehr wünschenswert, die gebundenen Stoffe mit dem Namen ‚Bindebatik' zu bezeichnen, die anderen mit ‚Wachsbatik'."[4] Loebèrs Kritik trifft insbesondere Stoffe, die unter der Bezeichnung „Batik" während der Kriegsjahre in deutsche Geschäfte kamen und solche, die von der 1917 gegründeten Berliner Firma „Deutsche Batiks" vertrieben wurden.

Die beiden herausgegriffenen Zitate aus der zweiten Dekade des noch jungen 20. Jahrhunderts deuten die Schwierigkeiten an, in denen sich die deutsche Batikkunst gegen Ende des Ersten Weltkriegs befand. Die in ihrer Anfangsphase gepriesenen hohen künstlerischen Ansprüche wurden im Laufe der Jahre durch die Popularisierung des Verfahrens und letztlich die Interessen der Industrie unterlaufen, die sehr komplexe Technik verändert bzw. stark vereinfacht. Das bisher unter künstlerischen Prämissen geschaffene Unikat wich nun immer häufiger einem in Lohnarbeit hergestellten Verkaufsartikel.

Wie enthusiastisch dagegen wurde das Batiken noch zu Beginn des 20. Jahrhunderts als eine neue künstlerische Technik, als eine vielversprechende Kunst gefeiert, von Künstlern und vom Publikum! Den Wandel aufzuzeigen, den die Batikkunst in Deutschland in dem relativ kurzen Zeitraum von 1900 bis 1920 erfuhr, ist das Ziel dieses Katalogbeitrags. Ausgangspunkt hierfür bildete die fast auf den Monat genau vor einhundert Jahren eröffnete „Niederländisch-Indische Kunstausstellung" im Krefelder Kaiser Wilhelm Museum.[5]

Als Quellengrundlage wurden sowohl die im Kaiser Wilhelm Museum verwahrten Akten zu dieser Ausstellung als auch die bisher kaum ausgewertete Zeitschrift „Textile Kunst und Industrie" der Jahrgänge 1908 bis 1920 herangezogen.[6]

In Deutschland war die Batiktechnik bereits einige Jahre vor der Krefelder Ausstellung von 1906 bekannt geworden. Im Oktober 1902 wurde das Kunstgewerbliche Seminar in Weimar unter der Leitung Henry van de Veldes eingerichtet. Der belgische Künstler kannte bereits javanische Batiken aus der Sammlung von Johan Thorn Prikker und vermittelte die Technik weiter an seine Schülerin und Vertraute Erica von Scheel, die später Batikkurse an der Kunstgewerbeschule in Weimar gab und für Paul Poiret in Paris arbeitete.[7]

Nach dem großen Erfolg der Niederländischen Kunstausstellung im Kaiser Wilhelm Museum im Jahre 1903, auf der eine große Anzahl holländischer Batiken gezeigt worden waren, kamen auf Einladung der Preußischen Regierung ein Jahr später niederländische Künstler als Lehrer an deutsche Kunstgewerbeschulen, wo sie ihren Schülern auch Unterricht im Batiken erteilten:

J.A. Loebèr Jun. ging nach Elberfeld an die Kunstgewerbeschule, Johan Thorn Prikker wurde eine ähnliche Position in Krefeld angeboten, und Jules de Praetere, ein belgischer Künstler, ging zunächst nach Düsseldorf. Später, 1910, wurde er Direktor der Kunstgewerbeschule in Zürich.[8]

Die Batiktechnik, die an diesen Schulen gelehrt wurde, beruhte auf den Experimenten des Haarlemer Koloniaal Museums in den späten 90er Jahren des 19. Jahrhunderts. Im Laboratorium des Haarlemer Museums hatte man erfolgreich versucht, Batiken mit in Europa verfügbaren haltbaren und lichtechten Farbstoffen sowie bestimmten Wachskomponenten herzustellen, um schließlich dem javanischen Verfahren ein qualitativ ebenbürtiges entgegen setzen zu können. Die niederländischen

Batiken – oder auch Haarlemer Batiken genannt – erregten im künstlerischen Umfeld der internationalen Stilbewegung sowohl in den Niederlanden als auch in den europäischen Nachbarländern großes Aufsehen.[9]

So verwundert es nicht, dass die präsentierten Batiken auf der Niederländischen Ausstellung 1903 in Krefeld reges Interesse hervorriefen. Für Friedrich Deneken, den Direktor des Kaiser Wilhelm Museums, war diese erste Berührung mit niederländischen Batiken wohl ein entscheidender Anlass, sich auch mit der Kunst der niederländischen Kolonie in Ostindien zu beschäftigen. Von dem Erfolg seines Unternehmens von Anfang an überzeugt, nutzte Deneken seine Verbindungen zu holländischen Museen und Sammlern und zeigte drei Jahre später die erste große Ausstellung mit indonesischen Kunstwerken in Deutschland.

So bedeutete diese im Oktober 1906 feierlich eröffnete Schau mit zahlreichen javanischen Batiken und anderen Kunstgegenständen den Beginn einer erstaunlichen Batikbegeisterung. Das Verdienst hierfür gebührte zweifellos Friedrich Deneken; darin waren sich die Experten einig.[10]

Der Krefelder Museumsdirektor beabsichtigte mit dieser einmaligen Präsentation deutschen Künstlern eine Gelegenheit zu geben, sich mit der bisher kaum bekannten Kunst aus der niederländischen Kolonie vertraut zu machen. Gerade die ausgestellten Batiken sollten nicht nur ihrer neuen Technik wegen studiert werden, sondern auch als künstlerische Inspirationsquelle dienen.[11]

Darüber hinaus konnten die „zahlreichen und verschiedenartigen Textilerzeugnisse" ebenfalls der „heimischen Industrie [...] manches Interessante bieten"[12]. Und nicht zuletzt erhoffte sich Deneken mit dieser großen Schau, „dass die Verbindungen, die durch die erste niederländische Ausstellung des Jahres 1903 in so erfreulicher Weise zwischen den benachbarten Niederlanden und dem Museum und der Stadt Krefeld geknüpft wurden, durch die gegenwärtige Ausstellung sich noch enger und vielfältiger gestalten würden"[13].

Nach einer Vorbereitungszeit von drei Jahren eröffnete am 5. Oktober 1906 um 12.30 Uhr der Oberbürgermeister von Krefeld im Beisein von vielen geladenen Gästen die „Niederländisch-Indische Kunstausstellung". Sie zeigte laut Pressemitteilung der Stadt „Erzeugnisse aus den niederländischen Kolonien Ostindiens: Werke der Plastik, Metallarbeiten, Waffen, Web- und Flechtarbeiten, Batiks, Wajangfiguren, Musikinstrumente u.a.m."[14] Anschließend wurde zu einem „Festmahl" gebeten, und der Abend sollte mit einer Einladung ins Stadttheater ausklingen, in dem Bizets „Carmen" zu hören war.

Anlässlich dieser Feierlichkeiten mit hohem ausländischem Besuch wurden für diese Zeit typische „Vivatbänder" gewebt und verschenkt, die die Ausstellung im Kaiser Wilhelm Museum bewerben sollten.[15]

Die Präsentation indonesischer Kunst in der damals finanzstarken Stadt am Niederrhein, die bis zum 4. November zu sehen war, schien gelungen, zog sie doch eine so große Zahl Besucher – auch aus dem Ausland – an, wie keine Ausstellung seit der Gründung des Museums im Jahr 1897. Der 72-seitige Katalog wurde als Führer durch die verschiedenen Bereiche konzipiert und von namhaften, zumeist niederländischen Experten verfasst.[16]

Der Erfolg der Ausstellung spiegelte sich vor allem in den Rezensionen zahlreicher Tageszeitungen und Fachblätter im In- und Ausland.[17] Das Urteil der Autoren über die ausgestellten javanischen Batiken fiel zumeist sehr positiv aus. Viele Rezensenten beschrieben ihrem Publikum das Verfahren und wiesen auf die für europäische Augen ungewohnten, fremden Muster hin, die einen „exotischen Hauch" über Krefeld legten.[18] Oftmals wurden die holländischen Batiken als Vergleich herangezogen, und man verwies auf die „Niederländische Ausstellung" im Kaiser Wilhelm Museum im Jahr 1903.[19] Diese niederländischen Batiken im Blick, sahen einige Autoren den „kunstgewerblichen Wert [...] in der Anwendung der Batiktechnik für die Bemalung von Decken, Vorhängen, Tüchern u.s.w. [liegen]" und nicht so sehr in dem Entwurf von Stoffen für die Modeindustrie.[20] Zugleich fiel die Bemerkung, dass das Batiken „in Europa zunächst noch eine

Kunst für die Reichen" sei, die von erfahrenen Künstlern ausgeübt würde.[21] Ein anderer Aspekt der Batiktechnik wird in einer Rezension im „Kunstgewerbeblatt" hervorgehoben: „Die Technik tritt als Anreger der Stilbildung [und nicht das Ornament, d. V.] in den Vordergrund, und so mag die Zeit gekommen sein, von uralten und sehr gesunden Techniken anderer Völker zu lernen."[22] Insgesamt wurde die Ausstellung im Kaiser Wilhelm Museum mit ihren zahlreichen außereuropäischen Exponaten als sehr ungewöhnlich – zum Teil als sensationell – und durchaus als willkommene Anregung empfunden.

Zur Ausstellung erschien neben dem von Friedrich Deneken herausgegebenen Katalog bereits im Oktober 1906 ein „Flugblatt", das man den Besuchern aushändigte. Diese als Begleitheft gedachte Broschüre war bereits 1901 erstmals vom Haarlemer Laboratorium verfasst und veröffentlicht worden und fand in den späteren Jahren in überarbeiteter Form nicht nur in den Niederlanden, sondern in ganz Europa große Verbreitung. Das „Vlugblad" erläuterte die Grundlagen der niederländischen Batiktechnik und referierte die Ergebnisse der Farbexperimente unter Leitung des Haarlemer Laboratoriums. Die Broschüre wurde im Laufe der nächsten Jahre in mehrere Sprachen übersetzt und kostenlos verteilt.[23] Die zur Krefelder Ausstellung rechtzeitig erschienene deutsche Version des „Vlugblads" enthält „das Batikfärbeverfahren nach Versuchen, angestellt im Laboratorium des Kolonialmuseums zu Haarlem, nach Mitteilungen der Direktion des Museums und zur Erläuterung der von derselben hergerichteten technologischen Batik-Kollektion auf der Niederländisch-Indischen Kunstausstellung Krefeld 1906".[24]

Im Vorwort wird die Batiktechnik mit dem Stoffdruck verglichen:
„Im Vergleich mit der Stoffmusterung durch Druckverfahren hat das Batiken erhebliche Vorzüge. Die Drucktechnik ist als mechanischer Vorgang an feste Regeln und Vorlagen gebunden, während das Batiken eine freie, individuelle Kunst ist. Mit dem Druckverfahren vermag man nur auf die Oberfläche der Gewebe einzuwirken, während durch das Färbeverfahren des Batikens die Farbstoffe in die Fasern der Gewebe eindringen." An das Vorwort schließt sich eine Übersicht der wichtigsten Batikfärbemethoden an: zunächst das „Blaufärben

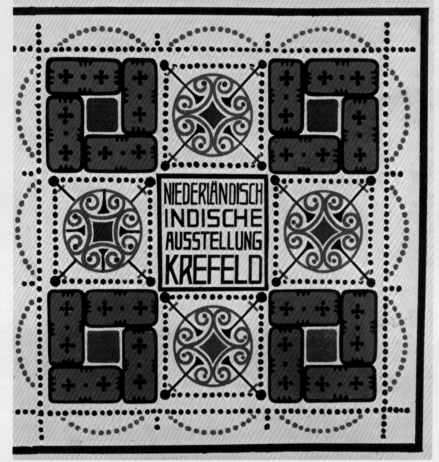

Zwei Jahre nach Ende der Niederländisch-Indischen Ausstellung in Krefeld zeigten sich erste Anzeichen für eine allgemeinere Verbreitung dieses neuen Musterungsverfahrens in Deutschland. Immer häufiger erschienen nun Artikel über Batikkünstler in Zeitschriften, wie beispielsweise in „Textile Kunst und Industrie". Diese Monatsschrift war 1908 gegründet worden, als „einziges Organ für das Gesamtgebiet der Textil-, Tapeten- und verwandten Industrien, das deren rein künstlerische Interessen vertritt". In der Einführung zum 1. Heft beschreiben Herausgeber Oskar Haebler und der Verlag das Ziel, das sich die Zeitschrift setzte, in folgender Weise:
„Sie [die Zeitschrift, d. V.] wird die bedeutenden Fortschritte verfolgen, welche die textile Kunstindustrie durch ihre Verbindung mit den schaffenden Künstlern erreicht hat, und bemüht sein, das Ergebnis dieses Zusammenwirkens in guten Abbildungen vor Augen zu führen. Dem Bilde das erläuternde Wort beizufügen, dafür sorgt die Mitarbeit berufener Fachmänner."[34]

Mit „textiler Kunstindustrie" waren sowohl die Sparte der Teppichindustrie gemeint als auch seriell – in Handarbeit oder maschinell – hergestellte Dekorationstextilien, denen ein künstlerischer Entwurf zugrunde lag.
Bereits im April-Heft desselben Jahres erschien ein umfangreicher Beitrag von J.A. Loebèr Jun. zu „Elberfelder Batiks, mit 14 Illustrationen nach Arbeiten des Verfassers und seiner Schüler, entworfen und ausgeführt in der Fachklasse für Buchausstattung und ornamentales Entwerfen der Elberfelder Kunstgewerbeschule".[35] Neben Entwürfen des Autors und Lehrers Loebèr sind auch Batiken seiner Schüler Gustav Bense, Emmy Rubens, Marta Barmé und Karl Reinhardts abgebildet. Die Beispiele zeigen nicht nur Entwürfe für Dekorationstextilien und Wandbehänge, sondern auch für Damenbekleidung, ein Schritt in eine neue Richtung, wie Loebèr betont: „Doch nicht nur auf dem Gebiete der Innenkunst liegen weite Felder für das Batiken offen! [...] Die vielen Mädchen aus besseren Kreisen, die jetzt das trostlose Heer der ‚Malweiber' bilden, finden hier ein angewiesenes Feld zur besseren, nützlichen Betätigung, die im schönen Sinne des Wortes zum ‚Eigenkleid der Frau' führen kann. Auf diese Weise schafft unsere Batikkunst in paralleler Richtung mit der alten Javanischen."[36] Ein Konzertkleid sowie eine aufwendig bebatikte Bluse werden dem Leser vorgestellt.
Zwei Jahre später erschien ein weiterer Artikel in der gleichen Zeitschrift, in dem Arbeiten Marta Barmés, vor allem ihre Kleiderentwürfe, gewürdigt werden. Die dargestellten Kleider, die teilweise sowie auch vollständig gebatikt sind, zeigen geometrische Ornamentformen – Kreise, Ovale, Spiralen, Sterne. Der Musteraufbau ist zumeist symmetrisch angelegt. Der anonyme Autor urteilt, dass „hinsichtlich der Farbengebung [zu sagen ist], daß die Kleider in Kirschrot und Graublau mit Braun einen vorzüglichen Eindruck erzeugen".[37]
Marta Barmé verließ Elberfeld im gleichen Jahr und eröffnete ein Atelier in Berlin, in dem sie ihre Batiken anbot.
Welchen großen Eindruck Batikkleider dieser Zeit in den hohen Gesellschaftsschichten hinterließen, bezeugen Zeitgenossen wie Loebèr, der berichtete, dass es Kronprinzessin Cäcilie war, die am Berliner Hof gebatikte Abendkleider einführte.[38] Eine andere Zeitzeugin, Helene von Nostitz, erzählt von den angenehmen und anregenden Besuchen im Wohnhaus „Hohe Pappeln" van de Veldes in Weimar in

ihrem Buch „Aus dem alten Europa", das 1924 erstmals erschienen war:

„Und ich entsinne mich noch, wie stark mein Eindruck bei einem Vortrag war, als um das schwarze
Klavier in dem hallenartigen Raum Frauen in der
Tracht und mit dem Schmuck der Zeit umher saßen,
den van de Velde selbst entworfen hatte. Exotische
Batikstoffe mit kleinen Halsausschnitten, meist
grüne Steine an einfachen langen Ketten, dazwischen die schwarzen Anzüge der Herren. Alle sta-
chen silhouettenhaft gegen die matten, ruhigen
Wände ab, auf denen einige Tänzerinnen von
Ludwig Hofmann die einzigen Farbflecke waren."[39]

Die vielen Kunstgewerbeausstellungen sowie die
steigende Zahl an Kunstgewerbeschulen im Land
ermöglichten es nicht nur dem Publikum, sich auf
den zahlreichen Ausstellungen in Museen oder
Kunstsalons zu informieren, sondern boten auch
Künstlern vermehrt Gelegenheit, ihre Arbeiten zu
zeigen. In den ersten Jahrgängen der „Textilen
Kunst und Industrie" wurde regelmäßig auf Arbeiten aus den Batikklassen verschiedener Kunstgewerbeschulen hingewiesen. Einige Schüler – vor
allem Schülerinnen – eröffneten nach ihrer Ausbil-
dung eigene Textilkunst-Ateliers. Im Hinblick auf
die Batiktechnik versuchten Künstler sowie
Forscher – auch an der Krefelder Färbereischule –
Verbesserungen zu entwickeln, angeregt durch die
zur damaligen Zeit herrschende „große Bewegung
zur Förderung der Qualitätsarbeit"[40]. Es galt, den
Ansprüchen nach Farb- und Waschechtheit gerecht
zu werden. In diesem Sinne boten Johanna Dedié
und Adelheid Postler in ihrer „kunstgewerblichen
Werkstatt für Innendekoration" licht- und wasch-
echte Batiken an, die mit der Bezeichnung
„Wachsschutzfärbekunst" auch begrifflich die
neuesten Fortschritte dokumentieren sollten.[41]

Bis zum Jahre 1911 gehörten Batiken in Deutschland zu „Luxusgegenständen [...], die durch die
besondere Sorgfalt, die ihnen gewidmet [wurde]
von vorneherein nicht als Ladenartikel in Betracht
[kamen]".[42] Die Situation änderte sich jedoch
schlagartig, als die Firma Albert Reimann in Berlin
einen so genannten Batikstift auf den Markt brachte, der das Batiken erheblich erleichterte: „Der ist
nun wirklich ein höchst kultiviertes und manierli-
ches Werkzeug geworden. Er verbrennt keine
Fingerspitzen mehr und macht auch sonst keine
eigenwilligen Mannöver. Eine Art Füllfederhalter
für Wachs, der nicht weniger tadellos funktioniert

[...]. Damit ist die Sache nun höchst einfach geworden. [...] Selbst die minderwertigste Begabung
kann ohne Schwierigkeiten damit wirtschaften und
jeder Geschmack [sic!] vermag so zu Wort kom-
men."[43]

Paul Westheim, der Autor des Artikels, prophezeite
eine „fundamentale Umwälzung"[44] für die Entwicklung dieser Textiltechnik. Damit hatte er wohl
Recht. Die Popularisierung der Batikkunst nahm
ihren Lauf, mit dem Reimann'schen Stift, der mit
Anleitung 7,50 Mark kostete[45], wurden weitere
Kreise von Batikinteressierten angesprochen, insbesondere Frauen, die für den eigenen Hausbedarf
batikten oder mit gebatikten Handarbeiten ihren
Lebensunterhalt aufbesserten.

Neben diesen privaten, für den Heimbereich gefertigten Batiken, gab es weiterhin die von Künstlern
sowie von Schülern der Kunstgewerbeschulen
gefertigten Arbeiten, die auf Ausstellungen gezeigt und in Zeitschriften besprochen wurden.

Wie beispielsweise Werke von Arthur Diener aus
Fürstenberg in Mecklenburg. Diener gehörte zu
den ersten deutschen Batikkünstlern, die sich vom
ornament- und linienbetonten Entwurf niederlän-
discher Vorbilder lösten. In seinen Wandbehängen
sind Einflüsse der internationalen Stilbewegung
und der japanischen Kunst erkennbar. Und in den
Dessins für Batikstoffe spiegelt sich zudem eine
Auseinandersetzung mit Arbeiten der Wiener
Werkstätte.[46]

Wiener Batiken waren ebenfalls Gegenstand einiger Artikel in der Zeitschrift „Textile Kunst und Industrie" in den Jahren 1913 bis 1915. Hervorgehoben wurden vor allem Arbeiten der Wienerin Else Stübchen-Kirchner, die an der k.k. Kunstgewerbeschule Unterricht genommen hatte und seit 1911 erfolgreich ihre Batiken im Museum für Kunst und Industrie (heute Museum für Angewandte Kunst Wien) zeigen konnte. Das Spektrum ihrer Werke reicht von gebatikten Stoffen auf Leinen, Seide, Samt und Baumwolle über Dekorationstextilien wie Kissenplatten und Vorhänge bis zu Kleidung und Accessoires. Die Entwürfe verraten einen deutlichen Einfluss der Wiener Werkstätte, lassen aber gelegentlich auch Anlehnungen an die niederländische Batikkunst erkennen.[47]

Else Stübchen-Kirchner verwendete für ihre Batiken nicht nur den *Tjanting*, sondern auch den Pinsel, mit dem sie das Wachs aufmalte. Die Künstlerin stellte ebenso wie auch weitere Wiener Batikkünstlerinnen 1914 auf der Deutschen Werkbund-Ausstellung in Köln aus, auf der ihre Arbeiten hohe Anerkennung fanden.[48]

Im Jahr 1915 wagte J.A. Loebèr einen ersten Rückblick auf die Entwicklung der Batikkunst in Deutschland, elf Jahre nach Einführung dieser Technik an westdeutschen Kunstgewerbeschulen. Nachdem bereits in den beiden Jahren zuvor zum wiederholten Mal die „Elberfelder Batiks" besprochen wurden, äußerte sich Loebèr nun selbst und rühmte die deutsche Batik allgemein in hohem Maß. Abgebildet sind ausschließlich Entwürfe von ihm und seiner Schülerin Hanna Müller. Die technischen Neuerungen, wie den „Wachszeichenstift" und die neu entwickelten Farbstoffe, würdigt der Autor als wichtige Schritte auf dem Weg zu einer eigenständigen deutschen Kunstform.[49] Die Vorzüge der Batiktechnik gegenüber anderen Textilkünsten ist für Loebèr offensichtlich:

„Sie [die Batiktechnik, d.V.] gestattet dem Künstler ohne viele technische Vorrichtungen farbig und ornamental zu wirken, fertige Arbeiten herzustellen. Er kann einen nüchternen, baumwollenen Stoff in Kunstarbeit umzaubern, schmücken und verschönern mit farbigen Formen. [...]"[50] Diese engagierten Worte eines Batiklehrers, der hoffnungsvoll in die Zukunft blickte, täuschen jedoch nicht über die Tatsache hinweg, dass Deutschland zu dieser Zeit in einen Weltkrieg verwickelt war. Wachs und Benzin, notwendige Materialien zur Ausübung der Batikkunst, galten als rare Güter, die einer Rationierung unterlagen. So war es nicht verwunderlich, als 1917 an der Stuttgarter Kunstgewerbeschule ein „Ätzverfahren für Batiks" entwickelt wurde, das im Wesentlichen auf die Wachsentfernung mit Benzin sowie auf größere Mengen an Wachs verzichten konnte.[51] Laura Eberhardt, Lehrerin an der Kunstgewerbeschule, beschreibt in einem kurzen Beitrag anschaulich, wie mit Hilfe des Ätzmittels Hydrosulfit und mit „verhältnismäßig geringer Mühe großer Farbenreichtum"[52] erzielt werden kann. Die Ätztechnik eignete sich vor allem für zweifarbige Stoffe, deren Musterung grob und nicht sehr kleinteilig war. Jeder mehrfarbige komplexe Entwurf dagegen erforderte große Mengen an Wachs.

Dieses neue Verfahren machte sich vermutlich die Firma „Deutsche Batiks" in Berlin zunutze; sie vertrieb seit spätestens 1917 Stoffe mit batikartigen Mustern, die teils gebatikt, teils in anderen Techniken hergestellt wurden. Darunter befanden sich sowohl Kleiderstoffe als auch Dekorationstextilien. Photographien von Stoffen dieser Firma lassen vermuten, dass viele Textilien in Wickelreservetechnik bzw. Nähreservierung entstanden (Plangi- bzw. Tritik-Technik), ohne Verwendung von Wachs.[53]

Im November desselben Jahres veranstaltete die Firma „Deutsche Batiks" in Berlin eine große Batik-Ausstellung, auf der verschiedene Unternehmen mit ihren Textilerzeugnissen vertreten waren. Diese Entwicklung hin zu einer deutschen „Batik-Industrie" wurde positiv bewertet, insbesondere für den Bereich der Mode, da sie „der deutschen Bekleidungsindustrie Gelegenheit gegeben [hat], eine öde Periode zu überwinden, in der nur einfarbige Stoffe auf den Markt kamen; ferner [...] hat sie den Anlaß zur Schaffung einer wirklich eigenartigen deutschen Mode gegeben."[54] Leider gibt es weder von der Ausstellung noch überhaupt farbige Aufnahmen, die eine Beurteilung der Qualität dieser Textilien erlauben würden.

Diejenigen Fotos aber, die einen kleinen Einblick in
die Welt der „Deutschen Batiks" gewähren, zeigen
sehr grob gemusterte Stoffe und Kleider, die über-
dies schnitttechnisch nicht viel Raffinesse vermuten
lassen.

Kurze Zeit später erhob J.A. Loebèr Jun. die Stimme
zur Verteidigung der „echten" Batik.[55] Der Elberfelder Professor mahnte an, den von der deutschen
Seidenbranche mißbräuchlich verwendeten Begriff
„Batik" nur für die im Wachsreserveverfahren hergestellten Textilien zu verwenden. Die fälschlicher-
weise so bezeichneten Stoffe seien keine Batiken
im strengen Sinne. Loebèr erinnert noch einmal an
die Geschichte der Batik in Deutschland, an seine
Verdienste und diejenigen seiner Kollegen und
hegt die Hoffnung, dass nach Beendigung des
Krieges, wenn wieder Wachs und Benzin zur
Verfügung stünden, die Batikkunst erneut zu einer
„Blütezeit" gelänge.[56]

An dieser Stelle ist nun eine Zäsur zu setzen. Die
Zeit nach 1918 birgt genügend Stoff für eine eigene Abhandlung. Die „echte" Batiktechnik geriet
nicht ins Abseits, wie dies einige Autoren befürch-
teten, sondern sie wurde weiterhin an den Kunstgewerbeschulen gelehrt. Die vom Deutschen Werkbund herausgegebenen Publikationen „Handwerkliche Kunst in alter und neuer Zeit" fügten 1920
einen Artikel über Batik ein.[57]
Inzwischen gab es auch ausreichend Literatur zu
diesem Thema, und die Bezugsquellen für Batik-
materialien wurden in Zeitschriften und Büchern
publiziert. In der „Deutschen Modenzeitung" fand
die interessierte Dame die Vorlagen für gebatikte
Kleidung.

In dem umfangreichen Werk „Die moderne Damenschneiderei" wurde dem Thema „Batik" ein
eigenes kurzes Kapitel gewidmet.[58] Die Autorinnen
preisen diese Technik als „eine der schönsten und
interessantesten modernen Frauenarbeiten", und
merken zugleich an, dass Batik wohl das einzige
Kunsthandwerk sei, das „von jedem ohne Vor-
kenntnisse oder Zeichentalent" ausgeführt werden
könne. Ihr Fazit lautet: „Batik hat ohne Zweifel
eine epochemachende Bedeutung in der heutigen
modernen Frauenbekleidung". Beigefügt sind dem
Artikel drei Entwürfe für Blusen mit gebatikten
Besätzen und Krägen, die sich stilistisch anlehnen
an Blusenentwürfe der Elberfelder Batikklassen.

Deutscher Batikmode nachzuspüren wäre eine dan-
kenswerte und interessante Aufgabe; fürs Erste
konnte hier die wechselvolle Geschichte der Batikkunst in Deutschland seit ihren Anfängen um 1900
bis zum Ende des Ersten Weltkriegs in groben
Zügen umrissen werden. Die Qualität der Batikarbeiten ist sehr unterschiedlich, wie man dies nach
den Abbildungen in der Zeitschrift „Textile Kunst
und Industrie" beurteilen kann. Hierauf konnte an
dieser Stelle nicht näher eingegangen werden.
Friedrich Deneken hat 1906 mit seiner Niederländisch-Indischen Kunstausstellung den wesentlichen
Anstoß zu einer Batikbegeisterung in Deutschland
gegeben. Ob eine Krefelder Ausstellung jemals
wieder eine solche Bedeutung erlangen wird, wird
die Zukunft zeigen. Vorerst zählen die historische
Bearbeitung und Auswertung der damaligen Ereignisse.

Anmerkungen:

1 TKuI, 12. Jg. 1920, Heft 4, S. 110: Batikarbeiten von Haensch und Ernst, Dresden.
2 Ibid.
3 TKuI, 11. Jg. 1918, Heft 3, S. 89f.
4 Ibid., S. 90.
5 Das KWM in Krefeld verwahrt die Akten zu dieser Ausstellung unter Vc Nr. 18 I - III, Vc 18a, Vc 18b (neue Aktennummerierung: Bde. 25 und 26); außerdem: Carl-Wolfgang Schümann, „Niederländisch-Indische Kunstausstellung", Krefeld 1906. In: Kaiser Wilhelm Museum (Hrsg.), Der westdeutsche Impuls 1900 - 1914. Kunst und Umweltgestaltung im Industriegebiet. Krefeld 1984, S. 153 - 157.
6 Diese Ausführungen erheben nicht den Anspruch auf Vollständigkeit, sie sollen vielmehr als Anregung für weitere Forschungen dienen.
7 Thomas Föhl u.a., Bauhaus - Museum. Berlin 1999, S. 22; zu Erica von Scheel siehe auch Isa Fleischmann, „Ab heute ist Jugendstil". In: Kölner Museums-Bulletin, 4, 1998, S. 36 - 41.
8 J.A. Loebèr, Das Batiken. Eine Blüte indonesischen Kunstlebens. Oldenburg 1926, S. 102; Maria Wronska-Friend, Javanese batiks for european artists: Experiments at the Koloniaal Laboratorium in Haarlem. In: Itie van Hout (Hrsg.), Batik. Drawn in wax. 200 years of batik art from Indonesia. Amsterdam 2001, S. 106 - 123, S. 122.
9 Wronska-Friend, 2001, S. 117ff.
10 Dies spiegelt sich vor allem in den Besprechungen der Ausstellung in Tageszeitungen und Fachzeitschriften im Jahre 1906 (Akte V c 18 II) und im Jahr danach sowie in späteren Artikeln in TKuI, z.B. 2. Jg. 1909, Heft 5, S. 197; Deneken hatte bereits in den Jahren zuvor Ausstellungen initiiert, die über Krefeld und das Rheinland hinaus für Aufsehen sorgten und nach Ansicht vieler Fachleute „für ganz Deutschland Bewegungen hervorriefen" (Die Rheinlande, 3. Jg. Heft 9, Juni 1903, S. 327).
11 Friedrich Deneken, Vorwort, In: Führer durch die Niederländisch-Indische Kunstausstellung im Kaiser Wilhelm Museum zu Krefeld 1906. Krefeld 1906, S. IV; zum Stil der niederländischen Batiken um die Jahrhundertwende und ihren Einfluss auf die Batikstile europäischer Nachbarländer siehe Wronska-Friend, 2001, S. 121ff.
12 Deneken, 1906, S. IV.
13 Ibid., S. V f.
14 KWM Akte Vc 18 II, Bl. 126a.
15 Deutsches Textilmuseum Krefeld, Inv. Nr. 01004.
16 Einleitung von A. W. Nieuwenhuis, Professor der Ethnologie, Leiden, Steinplastik von E. A. Saher, Direktor des Museums voor Kunstnijverheid, Haarlem, Schnitzarbeiten von A. W. Nieuwenhuis, Metallarbeiten von M. Tonnet, Waffen nach J. D. E. Schmeltz, Batikarbeiten von C. P. Rouffaer, Gewebe- und Flechtarbeiten nach J.A. Loebèr Jun., Wajangspiel von M. Tonnet, Musikinstrumente nach Veth.
17 KWM Akte Vc 18a; es erschien sogar ein Beitrag über die Ausstellung in der nordamerikanischen Zeitschrift „Musical America", New York, 16.3.1907.
18 Frankfurter Zeitung, 16.10.1906, Nr. 286, Feuilleton: Die Niederländisch-Indische Ausstellung in Krefeld.
19 Zu dieser Ausstellung waren Besprechungen in Fachzeitungen erschienen, welche die Batiktechnik bereits mehr oder weniger ausführlich und genau erklärten, z. B. R. Breuer, Batiks. In: Kunst und Handwerk 54, 1903/1904, S. 336 - 339; Niederländische Kunstausstellung im Kaiser-Wilhelm-Museum zu Krefeld. In: Die Rheinlande, 3. Jg. Heft 9, Juni 1903, S. 327 - 334, bes. S. 327f.
20 Frankfurter Zeitung, 16.10.1906, Nr. 286. Dass sich die Batiktechnik nicht für Bekleidungsentwürfe eignete, sollte sich bereits einige Jahre später als eine Fehleinschätzung erweisen.
21 Ibid.
22 Anna L. Plehn, Die Niederländisch-Indische Ausstellung in Krefeld, In: Kunstgewerbeblatt, 23. Jg. Neue Folge, Bd. XVIII, Heft 2, Nov. 1906, S. 25 - 34, S. 25.
23 Wronska-Friend, 2001, S. 117ff.
24 23. Flugblatt des KWM, Oktober 1906, neun Seiten, nicht paginiert.
25 Ibid. S. 8f. Es wird hier allerdings verschwiegen, dass die Rotfärbung von Baumwolle mit alizarinhaltigem Farbstoff, die in Europa seit langem bekannt ist, nur gute Ergebnisse im heißen - und nicht im kalten - Farbbad erreicht. Siehe Wronska-Friend, 2001, S. 113ff.

26 23. Flugblatt des KWM, 1906, S. 9.
27 KWM Akte Vc 18 III, Blatt 101.
28 KWM Akte Vc 18 III, Blatt 168; eine solche Ausstellung hat im Kaiser Wilhelm Museum nie stattgefunden.
29 KWM Akte Vc 18 III, Bl. 102.
30 KWM Akte Vc 18 III, unnum. Bl.
31 Sabine Teubner, Manfred Osthaus, Die Restaurierung des Hohenhofs. In: Birgit Schulte (Hrsg.), Henry van de Velde in Hagen, Hagen o. J., S. 214 - 220, S. 218.
32 A. Steinmann, Zur Entwicklung der Batikdruckerei in Holland und in der Schweiz. In: Ciba - Rundschau 68, 1946, S. 2564f.
33 Erica von Scheel arbeitete zwischen 1910 und 1912 für den Modezar Paul Poiret in Paris, für den sie Batikentwürfe schuf. Werke aus dieser Zeit von ihr waren im November 1911 im Hagener Folkwang - Museum zu sehen. Siehe: Henry van de Velde, Récit de ma vie. Bd. 2: 1910 - 1917. Hrsg. von Anne van Loo. Brüssel 1995, S. 267 - 269, bes. 269, Ulrike Ittershagen, Ausstellungen im Folkwang - Museum mit Beteiligung Henry van de Veldes. In: Schulte, o. J. (s. Anm. 31), S. 307: 1. November - 31. November 1911; s. a. S. 308, November 1915; Klaus-Jürgen Sembach, Birgit Schulte (Hrsg.), Henry van de Velde, Ein europäischer Künstler seiner Zeit. Köln 1992, S. 114.
34 TKuI, 1. Jg. 1908 Heft 1, S. 2; zu den „Fachmännern" zählten neben anderen auch Friedrich Deneken.
35 TKuI, 1. Jg. 1908, Heft 4, S. 153 - 161.
36 Ibid., S. 160.
37 TKuI, 1910, 3. Jg. Heft 9, S. 369.
38 Loebèr, 1926, S. 102.
39 Helene von Nostitz, Aus dem alten Europa. Menschen und Städte. Leipzig 1933, S. 94, zitiert in: Thomas Föhl (Hrsg.), Henry van de Velde in Weimar. Das Haus unter den hohen Pappeln. Weimar 1999, S. 77.
40 TKuI, 3. Jg. 1910, Heft 7, S. 269.
41 Ibid.
42 TKuI, 4. Jg. 1911, Heft 6, S. 231.
43 TKuI, 4. Jg. 1911, Heft 2, S. 55.
44 Ibid., S. 56.
45 Ibid., Anzeige, S. 86; ein Batikkasten mit allem Zubehör bei Reimann kostete 16 Mark.
46 TKuI, 2. Jg. 1909, Heft 5, S. 197 - 204; Paul Schulze, Direktor der Gewebesammlung Krefeld und Autor des Artikels, verweist auf die laufende Ausstellung mit Batiken von Arthur Diener in der Gewebesammlung; TKuI, 6. Jg. 1913, Heft 1, S. 1 - 7; das KWM besitzt einige Batikstoffe von Arthur Diener – Musterproben –, die Friedrich Deneken für das Haus erworben hat.
47 TKuI, 6. Jg. 1913, S. 466 - 473.
48 TKuI, 8. Jg. 1915, Heft 1, S. 28 - 31; außerdem TKuI, 7. Jg. 1914, Heft 2, S. 45 - 62, bes. S. 62: Karl Walde, Ausstellung österreichischer Kunstgewerbe 1913 - 1914, Wien.
49 TKuI, 8. Jg. 1915, Heft 10, S. 358 - 371, S. 360: „In technischer Beziehung hat unsere deutsche Batiktechnik die Urtechnik schon längst überholt."
50 Ibid., S. 369.
51 TKuI, 10. Jg. 1917, Heft 3, S. 77, Abb. S. 84 - 89.
52 Ibid.
53 TKuI, 10. Jg. 10, 1917, Heft 3, S. 96 - 99, S. 111f.: Ernst Collin, Deutsche Batiks.
54 TKuI, 10. Jg., 1917, Heft 6, S. 218; Abb. S. 207 - 209.
55 TKuI, 11. Jg. 1918, Heft 3, S. 89f. siehe Beginn dieses Beitrags.
56 Ibid., S. 90.
57 Carl Rade: Batik. In: Handwerkliche Kunst in alter und neuer Zeit. Hrsg. vom Deutschen Werkbund, Berlin 1920, S. 49 - 50. Um diese Zeit begann auch Friedrich Adler, sich mit dem Batikverfahren genauer vertraut zu machen. Bereits einige Jahre später, 1924, wurde Adler ein Patent für die Entwicklung eines Wachsreservedruckverfahrens erteilt. Siehe: Jutta Zander-Seidel, Friedrich Adler – Textilien. In: Brigitte Leonhardt u.a., (Hrsg.), Spurensuche: Friedrich Adler zwischen Jugendstil und Art Déco. Stuttgart 1994, S. 292 - 343, S. 299.
58 Hermine Bartesch, Mathilde Fiedler, Die moderne Damenschneiderei in Wort und Bild. Leipzig o. J. [ca. 1919], S. 320 - 322.

Abkürzungen:
KWM   Kaiser Wilhelm Museum Krefeld
TKuI   Textile Kunst und Industrie, Jg. 1, 1908, Heft 1 ff.

Court official and his spouse.
Yogyakarta, c. 1920.

A SENSE OF THE EXOTIC IN KREFELD

The 1906 Dutch East Indian Art Exhibition in Krefeld and German Batiks until 1920

Isa Fleischmann-Heck

"Salome": Batik, wall hanging, by Gustav Bense, student at the Elberfeld school of arts and crafts, 1908

"Salome": Gebatikter Wandbehang, Entwurf und Ausführung: Gustav Bense, Schüler der Elberfelder Kunstgewerbeschule, 1908

In the April 1920 edition of the magazine "Textile Kunst und Industrie", an unidentifiable author with the initials H.B. makes a desperate plea to the German "batik community", asking it to counteract the "impoverishment of the art of batik" by bringing in "artistic influences".[1] A few lines previously he gives a detailed account of the evil referred to by him:

"Today, batiks are not just popular with the general public, among whom this revived technique has suffered an almost devastating stylistic decline in all its many useful but also absurd applications, it has moreover roused the interest of manufacturers [...]. Just as pokerwork was once considered a suitable activity for young girls, batik dyeing is now absolutely de rigueur. There is simple no way to control this evil [...] ." But on the whole, we can at least be grateful to artists who have made sure that "this fine technique, which in the right hands and guided by an imaginative mind is surprisingly versatile, has not been completely monopolised by amateurish, commercially minded, people." For this reason the author's appeal is directed above all at those artists who managed to resist the tempting offers of manufacturers.[2]

These agitated remarks by a critical observer were not the only comments betraying disappointment about certain "aberrant developments" since the batik technique had been introduced in Germany around 1900. Two years previously, in the March 1918 edition of the same publication, an extremely outraged J.A. Loebèr Jun., professor at the School of Applied Art in Elberfeld and batik expert and artist from the Netherlands, published a two-page article briefly entitled "Batik". In this article he expresses his disgust with the unscrupulous appropriation of the term batik on the part

of industry, using it for silk fabrics decorated in the tritik or the plangi technique.[3] According to the disheartened author, this use of the term batik is "particularly embarrassing in view of German thoroughness". "The trade has adopted the term 'batik' as its slogan, and enough experience tells us that this kind of thing is impossible to shift. [...] It would therefore be greatly preferable to describe these tie-dyed materials as 'tie-dye batik' and the others as 'wax batik'".[4] Loebèr's criticism applies especially to fabrics labelled 'batik' that entered the shops in Germany during the war years and those sold by the company "Deutsche Batiks", founded in Berlin in 1917.

These two singled-out quotations from the second decade of the early 20th century are indicative of the difficult situation in which German batik art found itself at the end of the First World War. Initially praised, the high aesthetic standards were over a number of years undermined due to the popularisation of the techniques and ultimately due to the interests of industry, which changed or rather extremely simplified this very complex technique. Artefacts that had been the unique products of artistic endeavour increasingly became commercial articles, produced by wage labour.

By contrast, at the start of the 20th century, the batik technique had been celebrated both by artists and the public as a new creative technique and a promising art form!

This catalogue contribution aims to illustrate the changes that took place in terms of batik art in Germany during the relatively brief period between 1900 and 1920. The starting point is the "Niederländisch-Indische Kunstausstellung" (Dutch East Indian Art Exhibition), which opened almost to the month one hundred years ago at the Kaiser Wilhelm Museum in Krefeld.[5]

The source material for this article are the records on the exhibition kept at the Kaiser Wilhelm Museum, as well as the little analysed editions of the publication, "Textile Kunst und Industrie", from 1908 until 1920.[6]

The batik technique had become known in Germany a few years before the 1906 Krefeld exhibition. October 1902 saw the foundation of the Arts and Crafts Seminar in Weimar under the guidance of Henry van de Velde. This Belgian artist was familiar with the Javanese batiks from the Johan Thorn Prikker Collection and taught this technique to his student and confidante, Erica von Scheel, who later ran batik courses at the Arts and Crafts Seminar in Weimar and worked for Paul Poiret in Paris.[7]

A year after the enormous success of the Dutch Art Exhibition at the Kaiser Wilhelm Museum in 1903, which featured a large number of Dutch batiks, Dutch artists arrived at German arts and crafts schools on the invitation of the Prussian government, where they also taught the batik technique: J.A. Loebèr Jun. went to the School of Arts and Crafts in Elberfeld, Johan Thorn Prikker was offered a similar post in Krefeld, and Jules de Praetere, a Belgian artist, initially went to Düsseldorf. Later, in 1910, he became director of the Zurich School of Arts and Crafts.[8]

The batik technique taught at these schools was based on the experiments undertaken at the Koloniaal Museum in Haarlem in the late 1890s. Batiks made with durable and lightfast dyes available in Europe and specific wax components were successfully produced in the laboratory of the Haarlem Museum, aiming to achieve a production method of the same high standard as that employed in Java. The Dutch batiks – also known as Haarlem Batiks – caused quite a stir in the artistic circles of the Art Nouveau, as well as in neighbouring European countries.[9]

It is therefore not surprising that the batiks displayed at the 1903 Dutch Art Exhibition in Krefeld created much interest. This first encounter with Dutch batiks appears to have been a decisive motivation for the director of the Kaiser Wilhelm Museum, Friedrich Deneken's own involvement with the art of the Dutch colony in the East Indies. Convinced of the success of his undertaking from the very beginning, Deneken made use of his connections with Dutch museums and collectors, and three years later he held the first great exhibition of Indonesian art in Germany.

Ceremoniously opened in October 1906, this exhibition of numerous Javanese batiks and other artefacts marked the beginning of an astonishing passion for batik. Experts agreed that Friedrich Deneken could doubtlessly take the credit for this.[10]

With this unique exhibition, the Krefeld museum director intended to allow German artists to become familiar with this previously little known art form from the Dutch colony. The batik exhibits in particular were not just meant to be studied for their technique alone, but also to provide creative inspiration.[11]

Furthermore, the "numerous and different kinds of textile products" would provide "much that is of interest" [...] "to the local industry".[12] Last but not least, Deneken hoped that this great exhibition would "strengthen and in many ways enhance the ties that fortunately were formed between neighbouring Holland, the museum and the town of Krefeld as a result of the first exhibition in 1903".[13]

Following three years of preparation, the lord mayor of Krefeld opened the "Dutch East Indian Art Exhibition" in the company of numerous guests on 5th October 1906 at 12.30 pm.

According to the town's press notices, the exhibition featured among many other things "products from the Dutch colonies in East India: sculpture, metalwork, weapons, weavings and basketry, batiks, wayang figures and musical instruments".[14] The opening ceremony concluded with a "banquet", followed by an invitation to a performance of Bizet's "Carmen" at the town theatre.

Characteristic of the period, "vivat ribbons" were woven to advertise the exhibition at the Kaiser Wilhelm Museum and presented at this ceremonial occasion, which hosted important foreign visitors.[15]

On show until the 4th November, the exhibition of Indonesian art in Krefeld, a then very prosperous town on the Lower Rhine, appears to have been successful. It attracted more visitors, including foreign ones, than any other exhibition since the museum was founded in 1897. The 72-page catalogue was designed as a guide to the different sections and written by well-known, mostly foreign, experts.[16]

The success of the exhibition is illustrated above all by the reviews of numerous daily newspapers and specialist publications both at home and abroad.[17] The authors' judgement of the Indonesian batiks on show was for the most part very positive. Many reviewers described the technique for their readers and pointed out the foreign designs to which they would have been unaccustomed, and which brought a "sense of the exotic" to Krefeld.[18] Dutch batiks were often used for comparison, and reference was made to the "Dutch Exhibition" at the Kaiser Wilhelm Museum in 1903.[19] In view of these Dutch batiks, some authors recognised a "crafts application [...] of the batik technique for painting items such as covers, curtains and cloths", rather than in the design of fabrics for the fashion industry.[20] At the same time it was mentioned that batik dyeing "in Europe would initially remain an art form for the rich", to be practised by experienced artists.[21] A further aspect of the batik technique was emphasised in a review published in the "Kunstgewerbeblatt": "The technique is primarily an inspiration for stylistic development [rather than pattern; author's note] and it may now be the time to start learning from the ancient and very wholesome techniques of other peoples".[22]

Overall, the exhibition at the Kaiser Wilhelm Museum with its multitude of non-European exhibits was perceived to be very unusual - in part sensational - and very much as welcome stimulation.

Apart from the catalogue edited by Friedrich Deneken, a "flyer" for the exhibition was available by October 1906, which was handed out to visitors. This brochure was intended to accompany the show. It was first written and published by the Haarlem Laboratory in 1901, and later editions became widely used not just in Holland but throughout Europe. The "Vlugblad" illustrated the basis of the Dutch batik technique and expounded the results of the dye experiments managed by the Haarlem Laboratory. During the course of the next few years, the brochure was translated into several languages and distributed free of charge.[23] Published in time for the Krefeld Exhibition, the German version of the "Vlugblad" deals with "the batik dyeing technique according to trials at the laboratory of the Kolonial Museum in Haarlem, based on notes by the museum management, as well as an explanation of the technological batik collection which it arranged for the 1906 Dutch East Indian Art Exhibition in Krefeld".[24] The foreword compares the batik technique with textile printing:

"In comparison to fabric design created by printing, the batik technique has considerable advantages. The printing technique is a mechanical process tied to fixed rules and patterns, whereas batik dyeing is a free, individual art form. The printing technique can only affect the fabric surface, whereas during the batik process the dyes penetrate into the fibres of the fabric." The foreword is followed by an overview of the most important batik dyeing technique. First, "blue dyeing with indigo", then "brown dyeing", followed by "parchment dyeing", "other plant dyes", as well as "red dyeing and the alizarin technique". The results of the Haarlem trials allowed the following conclusions: "1. It is not recommended to use aniline dyes, not even the best quality ones, for batik dyeing on cotton, silk and wool. [...] 2. Alizarin dyes are highly recommended, both for dyeing cotton and silk; they have excellent light and colourfastness."[25]

The authors conclude their explanations with the unequivocal statement:

"The batik technique is not suited for factory-based application. Submitted to the demands of industrial production, it would lose its true character. It does not tolerate mechanical processes and division of labour. Batiks have to be created by living independent producers. Only then will they show the particular characteristics inherent in the original technique. [...] May many people be inspired to practise the batik technique independently and creatively and to enrich contemporary art with this new technique, which will be able to bear fruit as rich as those of Javanese batik itself!"[26]

In the Netherlands, batik artists had been enjoying great international success for several years. So, what happened following the end of this unique exhibition, both in Krefeld and elsewhere in Germany?

Initially, the enormous success of the exhibition was evident from the large visitor numbers in the month of October. At that time, Friedrich Deneken was already hatching new plans. He suggested a similar exhibition in Berlin, at the Kunstgewerbemuseum, and his request was welcomed by Wilhelm von Bode and by the director of the Kunstgewerbemuseum, Otto von Falke.[27] But no exhibition of this kind ever took place in Berlin. There may have been several reasons for this. In a letter dated 4th August 1908, Deneken informs a colleague of the challenge of this project – in consequence of the rejection from Berlin – however, he continues to speculate about a "Javanese export exhibition", featuring samples of timber and dyes used in the batik technique. The purpose of the exhibition was "of course, to find a market for these things in Germany".[28]

Deneken drew on the great commercial success during the Dutch East Indian Art Exhibition and the period following it. Such textiles and in particular cantings sold well both to industrial companies – such as Farbwerke Hoechst in Frankfurt – and to private individuals.[29] The cantings, provided by the Koloniaal Museum in Haarlem, cost 0.50 mark each. In the four weeks leading up to the end of the exhibition all seventy cantings were sold.

Subsequently, Deneken received a number of written requests with regard to the batik technique, dye sources, cantings and fabrics. The assiduous museum director tried to encourage Krefeld dye businesses to "stock everything required for the batik technique".[30]

The same year, in 1906, construction began of the "Hohenhof", the residence of Karl Ernst Osthaus. Osthaus commissioned the Belgian artist Henry van de Velde living in Weimar as architect. Batik fabrics graced several rooms of the "Hohenhof", as wall hangings, curtains and furnishing fabrics. During extensive restoration work of the house, it was possible to identify the discovered textile remnants as printed batik imitations, probably of Dutch provenance.[31] Such so-called batik prints were produced both in Holland and in Switzerland since the mid-19th century and exported to India and the Indonesian islands. The largest Dutch factories producing batik prints were located in Rotterdam, Haarlem and Helmond.[32]

Henry van de Velde was appointed director of the "Kunstgewerbeschule" in Weimar, which opened to students in October 1907. His colleague and student, Erica von Scheel, who ran a private workshop for textile art, began offering batik courses in 1908.[33]

Two years after the end of the Dutch East Indian Art Exhibition in Krefeld it was possible to see the first signs that this new design technique had become increasingly popular in Germany. A growing number of articles on batik artists appeared in publications such as "Textile Kunst und Industrie". This monthly journal had been founded in 1908 as the "only voice of the entire industry of textiles, wall paper and related arts that represents purely their creative interests". The publishing company and editor, Oskar Haebler, described the aim of the publication in the introduction of the 1st edition:

"It [the publication; author's note] intends to track important progress made by the textile art industry as a result of its association with creative artists, and to try and show the achievements of this cooperation with the aid of high-quality illustrations. Invited experts will complement the illustrations with explanatory text."[34]

"The textile art industry" was also meant to include the carpet industry as well as serial production – either by hand or machine – of decorative textiles based on artists' designs.

A comprehensive article by J.A. Loebèr Jun. had appeared in the April edition of the same year, on "Elberfeld batiks, featuring 14 illustrations, based on works by the author and his pupils, designed and produced by the book design and ornamental design class of the Elberfeld School of Arts and

Crafts".[35] The illustrations feature designs by the author and teacher, Loebèr, as well as batiks by his students, Gustav Bense, Emmy Rubens, Marta Barmé and Karl Reinhardts. The examples showed designs for decorative textiles and wall hangings, but also for women's clothing, a step in a new direction, according to Loebèr: "The batik technique offers great opportunities, and not just in interior design! [...] The many girls from good families, who now make up the dreary army of 'painting wenches', can make use of these instructions to find a better, more useful occupation, which in the best sense of the word would make it possible for women to create their 'Eigenkleid' (reform dress). In this sense our batik art form works in tandem with that of the ancient Javanese."[36] The reader is shown a concert dress and a blouse with elaborate batik design.

Two years later, a further article appeared in the same publication, highlighting the work of Marta Barmé, and in particular her dress designs. The illustrated dresses, which in part were completely made in the batik technique, depict geometric designs - circles, ovals, spirals, stars. The design layout tends to be symmetrical. The anonymous author concludes that "in terms of colour, the dresses in cherry red and grey-blue and brown create an excellent impression".[37]

The same year, Marta Barmé left Elberfeld and opened a studio in Berlin, where she offered her batiks for sale.

The great impression made on the upper classes by the batik dresses of this period, is recorded by contemporaries like Loebèr, who stated that the Crown Princess Cäcilie introduced batik evening wear at the Berlin Court.[38] Another contemporary witness, Helene von Nostitz, mentions the pleasant and inspiring visits to van de Velde's "Hohe Pappeln" residence in Weimar in her book "Aus dem alten Europa", which was first published in 1924:

"And I still remember the strong impression made on me during a lecture, by women gathered around the black piano in the hall-like room, who were wearing the dress and jewellery of the period, designed by van de Velde himself. Exotic batik fabrics with high necklines, and mostly green stone pendants hanging from simple long chains, interspersed with the black suits of the gentlemen. They all formed silhouette-like contrasts against the matt, calm walls, on which a few dancers by Ludwig Hofmann created the only spots of colour."[39]

The many exhibitions of applied art and increasing number of applied art schools in Germany allowed both the public to discover information at numerous exhibitions in museums and art salons and repeatedly offered artists the chance to exhibit their work. In its first volumes, "Textile Kunst und Industrie" regularly featured the work of batik courses at various applied art schools. Some of the students -above all female students - opened their own textile studios following their graduation. Artists as well as researchers - including those at the Krefeld Dyeing School - attempted to develop improvements of the batik technique, inspired by the then dominant "great movement for the promotion of high quality workmanship"[40]. The aim was to meet demand for colourfastness. In this spirit, Johanna Dedié and Adelheid Postler sold lightfast and colourfast batiks in their "arts and crafts workshop for interior design", whose "wax resist dyed" label was meant to document the latest advances in the technique.[41]

Until 1911, batiks were "luxury items" in Germany, "which due to the special care given to [their production] were from the outset unsuitable as mass produced goods".[42] But the situation changed dramatically once the company Albert Reimann in Berlin brought a so-called batik pen onto the market, which made the process of batik dyeing significantly easier: "This really is a most accomplished and compliant tool. Finger tips are no longer in danger of being burnt and no erratic manoeuvres result from using this pen. It is a kind of fountain pen for wax, which works no less flawlessly [...]. This has made such work incredibly simple. [...] Merely the smallest amount of skill is required to administer it, and every kind of taste [sic!] can be expressed."[43]

The author of this article, Paul Westheim, prophesied a "fundamental revolution"[44] in the development of this textile technique. He appears to have been right. The popularisation of the batik technique took its course, the Reimann pen, which cost 7.50 marks including instructions[45], appealed to large numbers of batik enthusiasts, in particular women, who either employed the batik technique for domestic use or raised their standard of living by producing batik craft pieces for sale.

Batiks (tablecloths and cushion covers) of Heinz Weber and H. Link, students at the Königsberg school of arts and crafts, 1909

Batikarbeiten der Königsberger Kunstgewerblichen Lehrwerkstätte, gegr. 1908, Decken und Kissen von Heinz Weber und H. Link, 1909

In addition to such private batiks made for personal use, exhibitions and magazine reviews continued to feature works created by artists and by students at arts and crafts schools.

There was the work of Arthur Diener from Fürstenberg in Mecklenburg, for example. Diener was one of the first German batik artists who moved away from the pattern and line-dominated designs of the Dutch standards. His wall hangings demonstrate influences of the Art Nouveau and of Japanese art. Furthermore, his designs for batik fabrics reflect his interpretation of works by the Wiener Werkstätte.[46]

In the period between 1913 and 1915, several articles in "Textile Kunst und Industrie" discussed Viennese batiks. They particularly emphasised the work of Else Stübchen-Kirchner, a Viennese artist who had been taught at the Imperial School of Arts and Crafts (K.K. Kunstgewerbeschule) and had been able to exhibit her batiks successfully at the Museum of Art and Industry (now the Viennese Museum für Angewandte Kunst) since 1911. Her work ranges from batik fabrics in linen, velvet and cotton, to decorative textiles such as cushion panels and curtains, to clothing and accessories. The designs clearly betray the influences of the Wiener Werkstätte, but are occasionally also indebted to Dutch batiks.[47]

Else Stübchen-Kirchner utilised cantings as well as brushes for wax painting in her batik work. Together with other Viennese batik artists, she exhibited at the 1914 exhibition of the Deutsche Werkbund (German Crafts Association) in Cologne, where her work was very well received.[48]

In 1915, J.A. Loebèr attempted a first retrospective of the development of batik in Germany, eleven years after the introduction of this technique at west German applied art schools. Two years previously, the "Elberfeld Batiks" had been repeatedly reviewed, and now Loebèr himself spoke out in praise of German batiks in general. The illustrations exclusively feature designs by himself and by his student Hanna Müller. The technical innovations, such as the "wax draught pen" and newly developed dyes, are commended by the author as important steps towards an independent German art form.[49] The advantages of this batik technique compared with other textile techniques are obvious to Loebèr:

"It [the batik technique; author's note] enables artists to create with colours and design without the need for much technical equipment and to produce finished works. They can transform sober cotton fabrics into works of art, decorate and beautify them with colourful designs. [...]"[50]

Such committed words of a batik teacher looking hopefully towards the future, did not however conceal that fact that Germany was involved in a world war at the time. Wax and petrol, necessary materials for the practice of batik, were rare goods and had been rationed. It therefore came as no surprise that a discharge method was developed at the Stuttgart Kunstgewerbeschule in 1917. This largely eliminated the need for removing wax with petrol and for large amounts of wax.[51] In a brief article, Laura Eberhardt, a teacher at the Kunstgewerbeschule, clearly illustrates how it is possible to achieve great richness in colour with the aid of the hydrosulphite caustic substance and with "relatively little effort"[52]. This discharge technique was particularly suitable for two-tone fabrics with coarse, large-patterned, designs. Multi-coloured complex patterns, however, involved large amounts of wax.

The new process appears to have been utilised by the Berlin company, "Deutsche Batiks". By 1917 it was selling fabrics with batik-like designs, which

25

were made in part in the batik technique but also in other techniques. They included dress fabrics and decorative textiles. Photographs of fabrics produced by this company indicate that many textiles were made in the tie-dye or the stitch resist dye technique (plangi and tritik techniques, respectively), without the use of wax.[53]

In November of the same year, "Deutsche Batiks" held a large batik exhibition in Berlin, where various companies displayed their textile products. This development towards a German "batik industry" was reviewed positively, especially with regard to the fashion industry, because it provided "an opportunity for the German clothing industry to overcome a bleak period during which only monotone fabrics were produced for the market; furthermore [...] it was an occasion to create truly individual German fashion."[54] Unfortunately there are no colour photographs, either from the exhibition or generally, that would have made it possible to judge the quality of these textiles. The available photographs that do provide a small insight into the world of "Deutsche Batiks" feature very coarsely patterned fabrics and dresses, which furthermore were not very sophisticated in terms of their cut.

A short time later, J.A. Loebèr Jun. spoke out in defence of "true" batik.[55] The Elberfeld professor urged that the term "batik", falsely used by the German silk industry, should only be applied to textiles produced in the wax resist dye technique. The fabrics erroneously described as such were not batiks in the strict sense of the word. Loebèr again reminded of the history of batik in Germany, of his efforts and those of his colleagues, and expressed his hope that after the end of the war, when wax and petrol would once again become available, the batik art form would reach a new "zenith".[56]

At this point this history breaks off. The period after 1918 provides plenty of material for a separate critique. The "real" batik technique did not pale into insignificance, as some authors feared, but it continued to be taught at arts and crafts schools. Published by the Deutsche Werkbund in 1920, "Handwerkliche Kunst in alter und neuer Zeit" (Ancient and Contemporary Crafts) included an article on batik.[57]

In the meantime, a large amount of literature had been published on the subject, and source references for batik materials appeared in magazines and books. The "Deutsche Modenzeitung" (German Fashion Magazine) featured batik clothing patterns for its interested female readership.

The comprehensive work, "Die moderne Damenschneiderei" (Modern Dressmaking for Ladies), includes a brief chapter on the subject of "batik".[58] The authors praise this technique as "one of the most beautiful and interesting of modern crafts for women" and mention at the same time that batik is probably the only kind of craft that can be practised "without any prior knowledge or talent for draughtsmanship". They conclude that "without doubt, batik is of epoch-making importance in contemporary women's clothing". The article is complemented by illustrations of three designs for blouses with batik applications and collars that are stylistically related to blouse designs of the Elberfeld batik courses.

It would be a both thankful and interesting undertaking to trace the development of German batik fashion. This is a first broad overview of the changeable history of the art of batik in Germany, since its beginnings around 1900 until the end of the First World War. The quality of batik artefacts is extremely variable, as is shown by illustrations published in "Textile Kunst und Industrie", but this is not the place to discuss this in any further detail. In 1906, Friedrich Deneken's Dutch East Indian Art Exhibition largely triggered the enthusiasm for batik in Germany. It remains to be seen if another Krefeld exhibition will ever achieve such importance. For the time being, what counts are the retrospective research and analysis of these historic events.

Women batiking. Java, c. 1890

Javanese men gambling. Java, c. 1885

Notes:

1 TKuI, 12th vol., 1920, issue 4, p. 110: batik textiles by Haensch and Ernst, Dresden.

2 Ibid.

3 TKuI, 11th vol., 1918, issue 3, p. 89f.

4 Ibid., p. 90.

5 The Kaiser Wilhelm Museum in Krefeld is keeping the records on this exhibition under Vc No. 18 I - III, Vc 18a, Vc 18b (new record numbers: vols. 25 and 26); also: Carl-Wolfgang Schümann, "Niederländisch-Indische Kunstausstellung", Krefeld 1906. In: Kaiser Wilhelm Museum (pub.), Der westdeutsche Impuls 1900 - 1914. Kunst und Umweltgestaltung im Industriegebiet. Krefeld 1984, pp. 153 - 157.

6 These comments do not claim to be comprehensive, but are rather intended as inspiration for further research.

7 Thomas Föhl a.o., Bauhaus Museum. Berlin 1999, p. 22; re. Erica von Scheel see also Isa Fleischmann, "Ab heute ist Jugendstil". In: Kölner Museums-Bulletin, 4, 1998, pp. 36 - 41.

8 J.A. Loebèr, Das Batiken. Eine Blüte indonesischen Kunstlebens. Oldenburg 1926, p. 102; Maria Wronska-Friend, Javanese batiks for European artists: Experiments at the Koloniaal Laboratorium in Haarlem. In: Itie van Hout (ed.), Batik. Drawn in wax. 200 years of batik art from Indonesia. Amsterdam 2001, pp. 106 - 123, p. 122.

9 Wronska-Friend, 2001, p. 117ff.

10 This is reflected above all in reviews of the exhibition in daily newspapers and specialist publications from 1906 (record V c 18 II) and the following year, as well as in later articles in TKuI, e.g. 2nd vol., 1909, issue 5, p. 197; in previous years, Deneken had already organised exhibitions that caused sensations beyond the borders of Krefeld and the Rhineland itself, and which according to many specialists "created movements for the whole of Germany" (Die Rheinlande, 3. vol. issue 9, June 1903, p. 327).

11 Friedrich Deneken, Foreword. In: Führer durch die Niederländisch-Indische Kunstausstellung im Kaiser Wilhelm Museum zu Krefeld 1906. Krefeld 1906, p. IV; see Wronska-Friend, 2001, p. 121ff. on the style of Dutch batiks around the turn of the century and their influence on the batik styles of neighbouring European countries.

12 Deneken, 1906, p. IV.

13 Ibid., p. V f.

14 KWM record Vc 18 II, folio 126a.

15 Deutsches Textilmuseum Krefeld, inv. no. 01004.

16 Introduction by A. W. Nieuwenhuis, professor of ethnology, Leiden; stone sculpture by E. A. Saher, director of the Museum voor Kunstnijverheid, Haarlem; carvings by A. W. Nieuwenhuis, metalwork by M. Tonnet; weaponry after J. D. E. Schmeltz; batik pieces by C. P. Rouffaer; weavings and basketry after J.A. Loebèr Jun.; wayang set by M. Tonnet; musical instruments after Veth.

17 KWM record Vc 18a; the exhibition was even reported in the North American publication, "Musical America", New York, 16/3/1907.

18 Frankfurter Zeitung, 16/10/1906, no. 286, Feuilleton: Die Niederländisch-Indische Ausstellung in Krefeld.

19 Reviews of this exhibition were published in specialist publications which had previously explained the batik technique more or less comprehensively and accurately, e. g. R. Breuer, Batiks. In: Kunst und Handwerk 54, 1903/1904, pp. 336 - 339; Niederländische Kunstausstellung im Kaiser Wilhelm Museum zu Krefeld. In: Die Rheinlande, 3rd vol., issue 9, June 1903, pp. 327 - 334, esp. p. 327f.

20 Frankfurter Zeitung, 16/10/1906, no. 286. The belief that the batik technique was unsuitable for clothing designs would turn out to be an erroneous judgement a few years later.

21 Ibid.

22 Anna L. Plehn, Die Niederländisch-Indische Ausstellung in Krefeld. In: Kunstgewerbeblatt, 23rd vol. new series, vol. XVIII, issue 2, Nov. 1906, pp. 25 - 34, p. 25.

23 Wronska-Friend, 2001, p. 117ff.

24 23rd flyer "Flugblatt" of the Kaiser Wilhelm Museum Krefeld, October 1906, nine pages, no page numbers.

25 Ibid. p. 8f. This does not mention however that red dyeing of cotton with dye containing alizarin, which had been known in Europe for a long time, only achieves good results in hot - and not in cold - dye baths. See Wronska-Friend, 2001, p. 113ff.

26 23rd flyer of the KWM, 1906, p. 9.

27 KWM record Vc 18 III, folio 101.

28 KWM record Vc 18 III, folio 168; no such exhibition took place at the Kaiser Wilhelm Museum.

29 KWM record Vc 18 III, folio 102.

30 KWM record Vc 18 III.

31 Sabine Teubner, Manfred Osthaus, Die Restaurierung des Hohenhofs. In: Birgit Schulte (ed.), Henry van de Velde in Hagen, Hagen, no date, pp. 214 - 220, p. 218.

32 A. Steinmann, Zur Entwicklung der Batikdruckerei in Holland und in der Schweiz. In: Ciba-Rundschau 68, 1946, p. 2564f.

33 In the period between 1910 and 1912, Erica von Scheel worked for the fashion czar Paul Poiret in Paris, for whom she created batik designs. Her work from this period was on display at the Hagen Folkwang Museum in November 1911. See: Henry van de Velde, Récit de ma vie. Vol. 2: 1910 - 1917. Edited by Anne van Loo. Brussels 1995, pp. 267 - 269, esp. 269, Ulrike Ittershagen, Ausstellungen im Folkwang-Museum mit Beteiligung Henry van de Veldes, in: Schulte, no date (see note 31), p. 307: 1 November - 31 November 1911; see also p. 308, November 1915; Klaus-Jürgen Sembach, Birgit Schulte (ed.), Henry van de Velde, Ein europäischer Künstler seiner Zeit. Cologne 1992, p. 114.

34 TKuI, 1st vol., 1908 issue 1, p. 2; the "experts" also included Friedrich Deneken.

35 TKuI, 1st vol., 1908, issue 4, pp. 153 - 161.

36 Ibid., p. 160.

37 TKuI, 1910, 3rd vol., issue 9, p. 369.

38 Loebèr, 1926, p. 102.

39 Helene von Nostitz, Aus dem alten Europa. Menschen und Städte. Leipzig 1933, p. 94, quoted in: Thomas Föhl (ed.), Henry van de Velde in Weimar. Das Haus unter den hohen Pappeln. Weimar 1999, p. 77.

40 TKuI, 3rd vol., 1910, issue 7, p. 269.

41 Ibid.

42 TKuI, 4th vol., 1911, issue 6, p. 231.

43 TKuI, 4th vol., 1911, issue 2, p. 55.

44 Ibid., p. 56.

45 Ibid., advertisement, p. 86; a batik box including all equipment cost 16 marks at Reimann's.

46 TKuI, 2nd vol., 1909, issue 5, p. 197 - 204; Paul Schulze, director of the Krefeld Textile Museum (Gewebesammlung) and author of the article, mentions the permanent exhibitions of batiks by Arthur Diener in the museum; TKuI, 6th vol., 1913, issue 1, pp. 1 - 7; the Kaiser-Wilhelm-Museum owns a number of batik fabrics by Arthur Diener - pattern samplers -, which Friedrich Deneken acquired for the museum.

47 TKuI, 6th vol., 1913, pp. 466 - 473.

48 TKuI, 8th vol., 1915, issue 1, pp. 28 - 31; also TKuI, 7th vol., 1914, issue 2, pp. 45 - 62, esp. p. 62: Karl Walde, Ausstellung österreichischer Kunstgewerbe 1913 - 1914,Vienna.

49 TKuI, 8th vol., 1915, issue 10, pp. 358 - 371, p. 360: "In technischer Beziehung hat unsere deutsche Batiktechnik die Urtechnik schon längst überholt."

50 Ibid., p. 369.

51 TKuI, 10th vol., 1917, issue 3, p. 77, fig. pp. 84 - 89.

52 Ibid.

53 TKuI, 10th vol. 10, 1917, issue 3, pp. 96 - 99, S. 111f.: Ernst Collin, Deutsche Batiks.

54 TKuI, 10th vol., 1917, issue 6, p. 218; fig. pp. 207 - 209.

55 TKuI, 11th vol., 1918, issue 3, p. 89f., see beginning of this article.

56 Ibid., p. 90.

57 Carl Rade: Batik. In: Handwerkliche Kunst in alter und neuer Zeit. Published by Deutsche Werkbund, Berlin 1920, pp. 49 - 50. Around this period, Friedrich Adler also familiarised himself with the batik process. Only a few years later, in 1924, Adler was awarded a patent for the development of a wax resist print technique. See: Jutta Zander-Seidel, Friedrich Adler - Textilien. In: Brigitte Leonhardt a.o., (ed.), Spurensuche: Friedrich Adler zwischen Jugendstil und Art Déco. Stuttgart 1994, pp. 292 - 343, p. 299.

58 Hermine Bartesch, Mathilde Fiedler, Die moderne Damenschneiderei in Wort und Bild. Leipzig, no date [ca. 1919], pp. 320 - 322.

Abbreviations:

KWM   Kaiser Wilhelm Museum Krefeld
TKuI   Textile Kunst und Industrie, vol. 1, 1908, issue 1 ff.

DE BATIKKUNST
IN NEDERLANDSCH·INDIE
DOOR
G·P·ROUFFAER·EN·D^R·H·H·JUYNBOLL

Cover of Rouffaer-Juynboll's classic book
on batik "De batik-kunst in Nederlandsch-Indië".
Haarlem/Utrecht, 1899-1914

JAVANISCHE BATIK

Die Kunst der Musterung mit Wachs

Maria Wrońska-Friend

Die indonesische Insel Java ist die Heimat der Batiktextilien – exquisite Stoffe mit Wachsreservemusterung, die allgemein als ein Bereich orientalischer Kunst in höchster Vollendung betrachtet werden.

Bei seinem Besuch in Java vor vielen Jahren zog die erhabene Schönheit dieser Textilien Rudolf Smend in ihren Bann. Zugleich war er erstaunt über die aussergewöhnlichen Fertigkeiten, die zur Herstellung solcher Stoffe erforderlich sind. Heute enthält seine Sammlung die besten Batikexemplare aus unterschiedlichen Werkstätten, die in verschiedenen Teilen Javas um die vorige Jahrhundertwende in Betrieb waren – eine Zeit, in der die javanische Batik technisch und künstlerisch ihren Höhepunkt erreicht hatte. Die Sammlung Rudolf G. Smends gilt weltweit als eine der wichtigsten ihrer Art an javanischen Batiken. Sie stellt eine wertvolle Quelle für das richtige Verständnis javanischer Textilkunst dar und bietet gleichzeitig einen Einblick in das soziale Leben und die ästhetischen Vorlieben der Hersteller und Träger dieser Textilien.

Batik in der Kultur Javas

Will man diese Textilgruppe richtig verstehen und schätzen, so darf man nicht vergessen, dass es sich bei der javanischen Batik um ein kulturelles Phänomen handelt, das in der westlichen Textiltradition kein Pendant hat. Außerhalb Javas betrachtet man Batikarbeiten zumeist als Stoffe von großer Schönheit, die man trägt, bewundert und sammelt, oder man schätzt sie als greifbaren Ausdruck hochentwickelter Handwerkskunst und spezialisierten Fachwissens – das Ergebnis jahrhundertelangen Experimentierens mit Naturfarbstoffen. Dies trifft zwar alles auf die javanische Batik zu, doch ist sie noch viel mehr: Es handelt sich um Stoffe, denen vielschichtige symbolische Bedeutungen innewohnen und die als sichtbare Äußerung javanischer Überzeugungen, Ethik und sozialer Ordnung dienen. Daher gelten Batiktextilien als eine der wichtigsten Ausdrucksformen javanischer Kultur.

Da diesen Textilien im sozialen und zeremoniellen Leben des javanischen Volkes eine große Bedeutung zukommt und die Herstellung der kompliziertesten Muster äußerste Konzentration erfordert, wird die Batik in Zentraljava nicht als Handwerk oder Kunsthandwerk gesehen, sondern als ein Kunstzweig in höchster Verfeinerung, genannt „halus". Die Batik teilt sich diesen hohen Rang mit der gamelan-Musik, dem Schattentheater *wayang*, dem javanischen Schauspiel und der javanischen Lyrik. Für Europäer ist interessant, dass zur „hohen" javanischen Kultur keine der bildenden Künste gehört, die in der westlichen Tradition allgemein als wichtigstes Medium künstlerischen Ausdrucks gelten, wie Skulptur oder Malerei. Stattdessen ist in Java und überhaupt im gesamten indonesischen Archipel die Textilkunst zum dominierenden Zweig der darstellenden Künste und zur Hauptausdrucksform der kreativen Fähigkeiten dieser Menschen geworden.

Auf einer anderen Verständnisebene dient die vielfältige Ikonografie der Batiktextilien als sichtbare Dokumentation der komplexen Geschichte Javas und des intensiven kulturellen Austausches mit benachbarten Ländern. Indonesien liegt am Scheideweg zweier großer Zivilisationen Asiens: Indien und China. Mindestens in den letzten zweitausend Jahren pflegten Gesandte, Händler und Repräsentanten der Regierungen beider Mächte regelmäßigen Kontakt mit den Inseln. Die indische Halbinsel übte einen besonders starken kulturellen Einfluss aus. Dies beweisen die Einführung der religiösen und künstlerischen Traditionen des Buddhismus und Hinduismus auf Java, zahlreiche Handelswaren – ganz besonders Seiden- und Baumwolltextilien – sowie Schrift und Literatur, z. B. die Sanskrit-Epen Ramayana und Mahabharata, die zur philosophischen und ethischen Grundlage der javanischen Gesellschaft geworden sind. Ebenfalls von Bedeutung waren die Handelsbeziehungen mit dem Nahen Osten, die im 16. Jahrhundert schließlich die Einführung des Islam, noch heute die dominante Religion der Insel, auf Java zur Folge hatten. Gleichzeitig wurden die Gewürze und andere Waren des indonesischen Archipels Gegenstand des Interesses mehrerer europäischer Länder, aus denen die Niederlande als Kolonialmacht hervorgingen und bis 1945 die politische Macht über die Inselgruppe ausübten.

Dieses bunte Mosaik kultureller Traditionen drückt sich in der Mustervielfalt javanischer Textilien aus. Die Oberfläche zahlreicher Batiken zeugt vom kreativen Geschick, mit dem uralte örtliche Traditionen harmonisch mit Musterprinzipien und Motiven aus der indischen, chinesischen, arabischen und europäischen Kunst vereint wurden. Die so entstandene machtvolle kulturelle Verschmelzung ist bis heute die Besonderheit der javanischen Kultur.

Im Laufe der Jahrhunderte hat sich die Batik auf Java in eine Vielfalt regionaler Stile entwickelt. Die Javaner und Sundanesen, die arabischen und chinesischen Einwohner Javas, die gemischte indo-europäische Bevölkerung sowie die Sultane und Bürgerlichen trugen früher unterschiedliche Arten von Batiktextilien. Die Mannigfaltigkeit der Farben und Muster führte zur Entstehung einer reichen Bildsprache, durch die das Batikgewand die ethnische und regionale Identität des Trägers oder der Trägerin zum Ausdruck brachte und die soziale Stellung, das Alter und selbst den Ehestand anzeigte. Batiktextilien werden bis heute als wichtige zeremonielle und rituelle Attribute verwendet, und erscheinen oft bei Feiern anlässlich neuer Lebensabschnitte – z. B. bei Hochzeiten, Beschneidungen oder Schwangerschaften – bei Ritualen am Hof des Sultans sowie als Opfergaben für die Göttin der Südsee, Ratu Kidul.

Die Ursprünge

Der javanische Begriff „Batik", der in den meisten westlichen Sprachen allgemeine Akzeptanz gefunden hat, bezeichnet sowohl das Verfahren zur Ornamentierung von Textilien als auch den fertigen Stoff. Die Batik ist eine komplizierte und aufwändige Textilmusterungstechnik, bei der heißes, flüssiges Wachs auf die Stoffstellen aufgetragen wird, die beim Eintauchen in ein Färbebad geschützt werden sollen. Wenn die Wachsschicht auf der Stoffoberfläche erstarrt, „reserviert" sie diese Stoffteile vor der Farbe – daher wird die Batikmethode als Reservemusterung bezeichnet (andere sind z. B. Ikat und Abbindetechnik).

Es gibt unterschiedliche Formen des Oberflächenfärbens mittels flüssiger Substanzen, die im Altertum wie auch in der Neuzeit in verschiedenen Teilen der Welt ausgeübt wurden und werden. Als Ursprungsort für die Erfindung dieser Methode wird meist Indien oder Ägypten genannt, doch das Färben mit flüssigen Reservemitteln wurde vielleicht auch unabhängig in mehreren Teilen der Welt erfunden. Manchen Angaben zufolge kam die Batikmethode von der indischen Halbinsel nach Java. Eine genaue Untersuchung der Geräte und Färbetechniken beider Regionen weist eher auf Unterschiede als auf Gemeinsamkeiten hin.

Das Wort „Batik" erscheint in europäischen wie auch javanischen Quellen erstmals relativ spät, nämlich im 17. Jahrhundert. Im heißen, feuchten Klima der indonesischen Inseln konnten Textilien nur selten länger als zwei oder drei Jahrhunderte überdauern, daher sind heute keine älteren Exemplare javanischer Textilien mehr erhalten. Die Theorie, dass sich die Batik auf Java relativ spät entwickelte, wird durch die Tatsache untermauert, dass die Reservemusterung mit Wachs auf Bali unbekannt ist. Diese Insel gehörte bis Ende des 15. Jahrhunderts, vor der Ankunft des Islam, zum javanisch regierten Majapahit-Reich und pflegt bis heute die Traditionen der indischen Kultur, die diesen Teil der Inselgruppe über ein Jahrtausend lang beherrschte. Die Reservemusterung mit Wachs entwickelte sich auf Java daher höchstwahrscheinlich erst spät, im 16. Jahrhundert, und ging vielleicht aus einer einfacheren Technik der Textilmusterung durch direktes Bemalen hervor.

Zeichnen der Wachsmuster

Das wohl hervorstechendste Merkmal javanischer Batiktextilien sind die klar definierten, präzise ausgeführten Muster, die mit flüssigem Wachs und einem kleinen Kupfergerät namens *canting* gezeichnet werden. Diese Geräte gibt es in verschiedenen Formen und Größen: Da sind die *cantings* mit feiner Ausflusstülle zum Konturieren des Hauptmusters, andere mit weitaus größerer Tülle zum Auftragen dicker Wachsschichten auf große Stoffteile, die ungefärbt bleiben sollen, und wieder andere mit sehr feiner Tülle zum Setzen winziger Wachspunkte (meist Füllmuster). Zum Zeichnen von parallelen Linien werden beispielsweise Doppeltüllen verwendet.

Das Auftragen des Wachses ist gewöhnlich Frauensache. Diese Aufgabe wird meist in Teamarbeit in spezialisierten Werkstätten ausgeführt. Jede Frau ist auf einen bestimmten Mustertyp spezialisiert: Die Erfahrenste zeichnet die anfänglichen Konturlinien und ist für die ganz feinen Füllmuster verantwortlich, die weniger Geschulten tragen dicke

Wachsschichten auf große Stoffteile auf, die meist den Hintergrund bilden. Die Ausführung der komplizierteren Kompositionen erfordert die Mitarbeit von drei bis vier spezialisierten Arbeiterinnen, die das gesamte Repertoire der Wachsmuster beherrschen. Die Werkstatteigentümerin beteiligt sich nur selten am Auftragen des Wachses. Ihr Part ist, die Komposition des Stoffes mit den speziellen Mustern festzulegen und die Teamarbeit zu überwachen und zu koordinieren. Bis heute werden in vielen Werkstätten die teuersten Batikarbeiten auf Kundenbestellung gefertigt.

Bei der einfarbigen Batik (in Java nur gelegentlich ausgeführt) wird der Stoff nur einmal mit Wachsmustern bedeckt und dann in einer Farbe gefärbt (Tf. 35). Nach dem Färbebad wird das Wachs durch Eintauchen in kochendes Wasser entfernt, und es zeigt sich ein helleres Muster auf einem dunkleren, gefärbten Grund. Bei mehrfarbigen Batikarbeiten muss das Wachs so viele Male aufgetragen werden, wie Farben vorhanden sind, wobei jedesmal ein anderer Stoffteil bedeckt wird. Da es keine Möglichkeit zur Fehlerkorrektur gibt, erfordert die Fertigung mehrfarbiger Batiken sehr viel Erfahrung und Vorausplanung.

Die Wachsreservierung wird auf Java von Hand aufgetragen, wodurch jeder Batikstoff zu einer einmaligen Kreation wird: Zwei mit den gleichen Mustern ornamentierte Textilien sehen einander vielleicht zwar ähnlich, sind aber niemals gleich.[1]

Eines der typischsten Merkmale javanischer Batik ist die sehr kontrollierte und disziplinierte Zeichnung der Muster. Nichts wird dem Zufall überlassen, und die Improvisation wird keinesfalls gefördert. Das Endprodukt soll so weit wie möglich der ursprünglichen Intention der Stoffherstellerin entsprechen. Es kann jedoch vorkommen, dass die Wachsschicht während des Färbevorganges reißt und die Farbe in den Stoff eindringen kann, wodurch eine unregelmäßige Äderung entsteht. Dieser Zufallseffekt, von europäischen Künstlern häufig verwendet und als typisches Merkmal der Technik anerkannt, wird in Java oft als technische Unsauberkeit betrachtet und vermieden. Vor allem das Reißen des Wachses beim Färben mit Indigo gilt als schwerwiegender technischer Fehler, der den Stoff untauglich macht.

Das Färben

Der Einsatz von Wachs als Reservemittel bedeutet, dass der Färbevorgang nur in einem kalten oder lauwarmen Färbebad stattfinden kann. Diese Bedingung schränkt die Palette der für Batiktextilien geeigneten Naturfarben erheblich ein. Im Prinzip wurden in der Vergangenheit in Java gewöhnlich nur drei Naturfarben verwendet: *indigo*, *soga* (Braun) und *mengkudu* (Rot). Diese Farbpalette mag sehr begrenzt erscheinen, doch die javanischen Batikhersteller und ortsansässigen Färber wurden wahre Meister darin, dieses Hindernis zu überwinden. Durch Variationen der Färberezepte und der Länge des Färbevorganges entstand eine umfangreiche Palette an Schattierungen und Abstufungen. Geschicktes Überfärben ergab ein größeres Spektrum verfügbarer Farben.

Indigo (*nilo*) ist der wahrscheinlich älteste und gebräuchlichste Farbstoff auf Java. Es handelt sich hierbei um eine oxydierende Farbe, die eine komplizierte Verarbeitung erfordert und wenig Spielraum für Fehler lässt. Um eine gute Farbqualität zu erzielen, muss der Stoff bis zu sechzig Mal in die Farbküpe eingetaucht werden. Der gesamte Vorgang kann bis zu zwei Wochen dauern.

Die braune Farbe (*soga*) stammt von einem Tanninfarbstoff, der aus drei verschiedenen Holz- und Rindenarten gewonnen wird. Die *soga*-Färbung ist traditionell mit Zentraljava verbunden, besonders den höfischen Städten Yogyakarta und Surakarta, wo einige Batikwerkstätten noch heute Naturindigo und *soga* verwenden.

Die leuchtend tiefrote Farbe (*mengkudu*) ist ein auffälliges Merkmal vieler Batiken von der Nordküste Javas, die um die Wende des 19./20. Jahrhundert entstanden (Tf. 23-31, 50, 51, 53, 56), und wurde gelegentlich noch bis Mitte des 20. Jahrhunderts verwendet. Es handelt sich hierbei um einen Alizarinfarbstoff, der aus den Wurzeln eines kleinen Baumes (morinda citrifolia) gewonnen wird.

Kandjeng Pangeran Ario Poerbonagoro,
military commander of the kraton of Surakarta,
with his wife. Surakarta, c. 1925

Wie *soga* ist *mengkudu* ein Beizfarbstoff und erfordert eine komplizierte Vorbehandlung des Stoffes. Der Färbevorgang selbst war ebenfalls langwierig und zeitraubend – der Farbstoff musste über drei Wochen lang mindestens einmal täglich in den Stoff eingerieben werden.

Die Anwendung von Naturfarbstoffen verlangte komplexe Fachkenntnisse aufgrund jahrelanger Praxis und Experimente. Die Färberezepte wurden nur selten notiert und gewöhnlich mündlich tradiert oder in der Praxis erlernt; in manchen Fällen waren sie nur der Werkstatteigentümerin bekannt und gingen bei deren Tod verloren.

Synthetische Farbstoffe, die auf Java ab Ende des 19. Jahrhunderts langsam aufkamen und heute üblich sind, erfordern weniger spezialisierte Kenntnisse und Ausrüstung. Zwar verringerten sie den zum Färben von Stoffen nötigen Zeitaufwand erheblich, doch ergab sich dadurch bei den javanischen Batikarbeiten eine einheitlichere Farbgebung, und regionale Unterschiede verwischten sich.

Die zur Fertigung eines Batikstoffes erforderliche Zeit hängt von verschiedenen Faktoren ab. Die wichtigsten sind die Komplexität der Muster, die Zahl der verwendeten Farben und der Einsatz von Naturfarben oder chemischen Farbstoffen. Die Fertigung eines zweifarbigen Rockes mittlerer Qualität dauert bei Synthetikfarben vielleicht vier bis acht Wochen. Bei Batikarbeiten höchster Qualität jedoch, wie sie zahlreich in der Sammlung Rudolf Smend vertreten sind, liegt der Zeitaufwand bei sechs bis acht Monaten täglicher Arbeit.

Batiken als javanische Kleidung

Batiktextilien wurden meist als Kleidung verwendet – als Röcke, Schärpen, Brust- und Babytragetücher sowie Kopftücher für Männer. Nur selten wurden Dekorationstextilien in dieser Technik hergestellt. Solche Stoffe wurden meist für die chinesische und indo-europäische Bevölkerungsgruppe produziert. (Tf. 59, 63-70).

Traditionelle javanische Kleidung erfordert keine Schneiderarbeiten. Sie besteht aus rechteckigen oder quadratischen Stoffstücken, deren Funktion durch die Größe und Art der Wicklung bestimmt wird. In den meisten Fällen wird die Batiktechnik zur Herstellung von zwei Rockarten verwendet: *kain panjang* und *sarong*.

Der so genannte „lange Rock" – *kain panjang* – besteht aus einem einzigen Stoffstück von etwa 1,10 m Breite und 2,5 m Länge. Der Rock ist gleichmäßig mit einem Musterrapport bedeckt (Tf. 1-11) und wird fest um die Hüften geschlungen. *Kain panjang* ist die offizielle Kleidung der javanischen Aristokratie und macht meist keinen Unterschied zwischen den Geschlechtern: Die gleichen Muster können von Männern und Frauen getragen werden.

Der *sarong*, ein schlauchförmiger Rock mit zusammengenähten Enden, kann als „kurzer Rock" bezeichnet werden, da nur etwas über zwei Meter Batikstoff dafür nötig sind. Er wird in Zentraljava als zwanglose Kleidung getragen und erlangte auch in anderen Teilen der Insel ausgesprochene Beliebtheit. Der *sarong* ist gewöhnlich mit einem markanten vorderen Feld namens *kepala* („Kopf") verziert, das ursprünglich zwei Reihen gegenüberliegender Dreiecke trug, das sogenannte *tumpal*-Muster (Tf. 24, 29, 31, 37). Später wurden vor allem bei den Batiken von der Nordküste Javas die Dreiecke durch Blumenarrangements ersetzt (Tf. 21, 22, 30, 43-54).

Heutzutage kombinieren javanische Frauen zwar Batikröcke mit geschneiderten Blusen (*kebaya*). Früher jedoch trugen sie ein langes, rechteckiges Stoffstück, genannt *kemben*, das fest um den Oberkörper gewickelt wurde (Tf. 13-17) und an zentraljavanischen Höfen noch heute getragen wird. Eine Batikschärpe – *selendang* – rundete die Tracht der Frauen ab (Tf. 23). Die formale Bekleidung javanischer Aristokraten wurde durch ein quadratisches Kopftuch – *iket kepala* – ergänzt (Tf. 12).

Die Batiktracht diente nicht nur als Gebrauchskleidung im Alltag und bei Festlichkeiten, sondern war auch symbolischer Ausdruck der Einheit gegensätzlicher Kräfte im Universum. Nach altem javanischen Glauben besteht das Universum aus entgegengesetzten Kräften, die ähnlich wie beim chinesischen System des Ying und Yang miteinander im Widerstreit stehen, sich aber auch ergänzen. Da Batiktextilien weich und geschmeidig sind und vorwiegend von Frauen gefertigt werden, stehen sie für das weibliche Element. Den männlichen Aspekt des Universums stellen der Dolch, der *kris*, und andere Waffen dar – harte, spitze Objekte, von Männern hergestellt. In der offiziellen Hoftracht Zentraljavas werden der Batikrock und der Dolch *kris* stets zusammen getragen, um die Ganzheit des

Universums symbolisch darzustellen. So wird das Kleidungsstück zum höchsten Ausdruck des kosmischen Gleichgewichts, in dem sich entgegengesetzte Kräfte vereinen, dargestellt durch Stoff und Waffe.

Die Batiken Zentraljavas

Die Batikkunst Zentraljavas lehnte sich stark an die Traditionen zweier örtlicher Fürstenhöfe an: die der Sultane von Surakarta und Yogyakarta. Diese Institutionen haben noch heute großen Einfluss auf das politische und kulturelle Leben dieser Region.

Die Sultane traten stets als Mäzene der lokalen Künste auf. Zwar werden heute am Hof keine Batiken mehr hergestellt, doch in der Vergangenheit waren Wachsarbeiten auf Textilien eine wichtige Beschäftigung der Hofdamen. Heute setzen die Ehefrauen javanischer Aristokraten diese Tradition in gewisser Hinsicht fort. Das Zeichnen kontrollierter, präziser Muster wurde zur Schulung persönlicher Eigenschaften wie Geduld, Konzentration und Präzision genutzt. Die Tätigkeit war zugleich auch eine Art Meditation mit dem Ziel, „die aufgestörte Seele zu beruhigen"[2]. Infolgedessen erreichte die Batik den Rang einer der wichtigsten Künste, und jeder Hof entwickelte eine charakteristische Farb- und Musterpalette. Eine Gruppe von Textilien in der Sammlung Rudolf G. Smend steht mit dem Palast von Yogyakarta in Verbindung und bietet einen hervorragenden Einblick in die Traditionen der javanischen Hofbatik (Tf. 1-3, 7, 8, 10, 12, 13-19).

Zentraljavanische Batiktextilien zeigen meist die blau-braune Farbpalette und heißen kain sogan (von soga, dem braunen Farbstoff). Am Hof von Yogyakarta erscheinen diese Farben auf einem frischen weißen Hintergrund, wodurch klar definierte Musterkontraste entstanden (Tf. 1 - 4). Am Hof von Surakarta bevorzugte man dagegen weichere, gelbliche Farbtöne (Tf. 5).

Manchen Batikmustern schrieb man besondere Kräfte zu, und Ende des 18. Jahrhunderts erließen die beiden Höfe Surakarta und Yogyakarta Edikte, wonach die Verwendung jener Muster den Sultanen und hohen Hofbeamten vorbehalten war. Diese Regeln werden an den Höfen noch heute eingehalten, und die Verwendung spezieller Muster kennzeichnet die soziale Stellung des Trägers oder der Trägerin. Die Gruppe der „verbotenen" (larangan) Muster enthält das atemberaubend schöne

parang rusak- („Zerbrochener-Dolch"-) Motiv, bestehend aus durchgehenden Wellenbändern, die in Diagonalreihen über die gesamte Stoffoberfläche verlaufen (Tf. 1, 8). Dieses prägnante alte Muster war an beiden Höfen ausschließlich dem Sultan und seinen engsten Angehörigen vorbehalten.[3]

Sawat ist ein weiteres Muster der larangan-Gruppe. Wahrscheinlich entwickelte es sich aus dem Palmettenmuster, einem der beliebtesten Motive in der Kunst des Nahen Ostens und Südasiens. Auf Java betrachtet man es als symbolische Darstellung des Garuda, des mythologischen Vogels, der einst den Gott Vishnu trug – eine beliebte Gottheit aus dem hinduistisch-javanischen Pantheon (Tf. 1 - 2). Ein weiteres, wahrscheinlich durch Handelsstoffe eingeführtes Muster ist das lar, ein tropfenförmiges Motiv, das in Indien buta genannt wird und bei der Ornamentierung von Kaschmir-Schals eine bedeutende Rolle spielt. Auf Java stellt dieses Motiv einen einzelnen Flügel des Vogels Garuda dar und war am javanischen Hof für Personen von niedrigerem Rang bestimmt (Tf. 12 - 13).

Kawung, ein altes, vierblättriges Blumenmotiv, ist bereits von den Kulturen des Indus-Tals (Mohenjo-Daro und Harappa, ca. 2500 v. Chr.) her bekannt und erscheint auf Java häufig als Musterung der Gewänder, mit denen Steinstatuen der Hindu-Götter und der als Götter verehrten Herrscher bekleidet sind. Am Hof von Yogyakarta galt kawung als larangan-Muster und erscheint auf Batiken häufig entweder als Hauptmotiv oder in Verbindung mit anderen Mustern (Tf. 2 und Foto S. 43).

Ein weiterer Favorit unter den Motiven zentraljavanischer Stoffe ist tambal, eine Ansammlung von Batikmustern, die einen Patchwork-Stoff imitieren (Tf. 4-7). Auch dieses Muster hat eine reiche Kulturgeschichte und steht mit den religiösen Traditionen Asiens in Zusammenhang. Buddha und seine Schüler erscheinen oft in geflickte Gewänder gekleidet als Ausdruck ihres Armutsgelübdes und ihrer Befürwortung eines entsagungsvollen Lebens. Im Islam trugen die Anhänger des Sufi-Ordens zerlumpte, geflickte Kleidung als Zeichen ihrer Verachtung für weltliche Güter. Ein ähnliches Kleidungsstück, die Patchwork-Jacke Kyahi Antakusuma („die verehrungswürdige Vielblumige") war ein Erbstück am Hof von Yogyakarta, und der Sultan trug dieses Gewand bei den wichtigsten Anlässen, z. B. beim Garebeg[4]. Die Javaner schrieben dem *tambal*-Muster heilende und schützende Kräfte zu, vor allem gegen Krankheit und das Böse, daher wurde es eines der bedeutendsten Batikmuster Javas.

Textilien mit gedruckten und gewebten Mustern wurden jahrhundertelang aus Indien importiert und hatten einen starken Einfluss auf den Musterstil indonesischer Stoffe. Das bedeutendste Handelstextil, das als der luxuriöseste indische Stoff galt, war die *patola*, ein Seidentuch mit Musterung in der hochkomplizierten Technik des Doppelikat. Aus technischen Gründen enthalten *patola*-Muster keine durchgehenden Linien, sondern sind aus winzigen, quadratischen, tropfenähnlichen Einheiten aufgebaut. In der javanischen Batik wandelte sich diese besondere Ornamentierung zum *nitik*-Muster (Tf. 6-8). Seine Ausführung in Wachstechnik stellt die Geduld und Sorgfalt zweifellos auf die höchste Probe und erfordert ein speziell konstruiertes *canting*.

Die Mehrzahl der Batikmuster für den zentraljavanischen Hof zeigt florale Formen in abstrakter geometrischer Stilisierung. Diese Ornamentierung reflektiert möglicherweise die Einflüsse islamischer Kunst. Einige Batiken weisen zwar kleine Tierfiguren auf, doch menschliche Gestalten fehlen. Der einzige Hinweis auf Menschen erscheint über die *wayang* Figuren des Schattentheaters (Tf. 9-11). Auf Java sind Auszüge aus den indischen Epen Mahabharata und Ramayana das beliebteste Repertoire des Schattentheaters und werden anlässlich wichtiger Ereignisse und Feiern aufgeführt. Das *wayang*-Motiv auf Batiktextilien erhielt den Namen *ciptoning*, und da *wayang*-Figuren für Weisheit und Erfahrung stehen, erscheint das Motiv auf den Röcken älterer, hochangesehener Personen bei Ereignissen wie Hochzeiten und Hofzeremonien. Für ganz besondere Anlässe erhielten Batikstoffe manchmal einen Goldauftrag, *prada* genannt (Tf. 11).

Three sons of the Rijksbestuurder of Yogyakarta and their payung bearer. Yogyakarta, c. 1925

Young man dressed in batik in front
of a table covered with a batik cloth.
Yogyakarta, c. 1925

Batikröcke der Gattung *kain panjang* werden bei
Hof und in der javanischen Aristokratie als offizielle Kleidung getragen. Bei ganz besonderen Anlässen wie z. B. einer Krönung oder der Garebeg–
Zeremonie trägt der Sultan einen *dodot* – einen
zeremoniellen Rock, der beinahe viermal so groß ist
wie ein *kain panjang*. Das Tuch wird um den Körper
gewickelt, wobei ein Ende normalerweise eine
lange Schleppe bildet oder eine Falte seitlich her-
unterhängt. Das rechteckige oder rautenförmige
Mittelfeld des *dodot* bleibt ungefärbt, nur die
Seiten sind mit wichtigen Motiven ornamentiert,
z. B. *parang rusak* oder *semen*, eine stilisierte Darstellung der heiligen Landschaft. Obwohl der
dodot eng mit königlichen Zeremonien verknüpft
ist, dürfen ihn Braut und Bräutigam an ihrem Hochzeitstag tragen. Nach javanischer Tradition ist das
frischvermählte Paar, auch wenn es einfacher Her-
kunft ist, an seinem Hochzeitstag „Königin und
König", und die Verwendung des königlichen Gewandes unterstreicht diesen Sonderstatus (Tf. 18-19).

Eine ganz eigene Bildsprache bestimmt die Verwendung des Brusttuchs *kemben*, das bis heute Teil
der offiziellen Frauenkleidung an den zentraljavanischen Höfen ist. Unverheiratete Frauen tragen
kemben des *byur*-Typs, die einheitlich mit einem
dekorativen Muster bedeckt sind (Tf. 13). *Kemben*
für verheiratete Frauen sind mit einem rautenarti-
gen Feld (*sidangan*) verziert – sichtbares Symbol für
den Status als Ehefrau (Tf. 14-17). Oft ist das Feld
mit sehr feiner grüner, blauer oder violetter Seide
belegt. Die Farben stellen keine persönliche
Vorliebe dar, sondern weisen auf die Situation oder
Zeremonie hin, bei der ein *kemben* verwendet
wird. Schwarz-weiße *kemben* (genannt *bangun
tulak*, Tf. 17) z. B. verwendet man als Schutztuch in
den verletzlichsten Lebenssituationen wie Schwangerschaft oder Krankheit, während grün-weiße
Brusttücher Opfergaben für Ratu Kidul darstellen,
der Göttin der Südsee und spirituellen Gefährtin
javanischer Sultane.

Bei manchen *kemben* wurde die Batiktechnik mit
anderen Techniken der Reservemusterung wie
plangi (Abbindetechnik) und *tritik* (Nähreservierung) kombiniert. Mehrfarbige Stoffe dieser Art
heißen *kain kembangan* („geblümter Stoff") und
stellen die interessantesten Exemplare der Frauenkleidung auf Java dar (Tf. 16).
Der *sarong*, ein schlauchförmiger Rock, wird in
Zentraljava nur als zwanglose Kleidung getragen,

doch selbst diese Stoffe zeigen manchmal interessante Beispiele von Batikmustern (Tf. 20-22). Das Repertoire an Mustermotiven ähnelt manchmal dem von formelleren Kleidungsstücken wie *kain panjang*, aber hier sind die Kompositionen freier gestaltet und nicht durch die Regeln des Palastprotokolls eingeschränkt. Das *kawung*-Muster vom Hof des Sultans ist z. B. durchsetzt mit Vögeln und Blumenranken (Tf. 22), während das *sawat*-Muster, ausgeführt auf einem Hintergrund aus frei gezeichneten floralen Arrangements mit Blumenkörben auf der Tuchvorderseite, den Einfluss der europäischen Ikonografie zeigt (Tf. 21).

Nordküste

Die Städte im nördlichen Teil Javas, *pasisir* genannt, entwickelten eine ausgeprägte Batiktradition. Die dortigen Küstenstädte treiben schon seit Jahrhunderten Seehandel, und es entstanden enge Handelsbeziehungen mit den Ländern des Nahen Ostens sowie Indien und China. Die facettenreiche Ikonografie der einheimischen Textilien reflektiert die ethnische und kulturelle Vielfalt dieser Gegend, in der große Gemeinden arabischer, chinesischer und indischer Siedler schon jahrhundertelang mit der javanischen und sundanesischen Bevölkerung zusammenleben. Eine weitere Gruppe mit eigener Identität waren die „Indischen", die gemischte indo-eurasische Bevölkerung – Nachkommen von holländischen, javanischen oder chinesischen Eltern, auf Java geboren und aufgewachsen.

Im Gegensatz zu Zentraljava, wo Batikmuster einst die soziale Stellung einer Person anzeigten, betonten die Textilien Nordjavas die ethnische Identität des Trägers. Die größten Zentren für die Batikproduktion waren Pekalongan, Cirebon, Semarang, Lasem, Kudus, Juana und Demak. Viele Batikwerkstätten wurden von nichtjavanischen Unternehmerinnen geführt – Frauen aus der Gruppe der „Indischen", von ortsansässigen Chinesinnen (auf Java *Peranakan* genannt), sowie von Araberinnen, die aus dem Jemen eingewandert waren.

Batiken aus Lasem

Zu Ende des 19. Jahrhunderts gehörte Lasem zu den größten Batikzentren in diesem Teil Javas und produzierte Stoffe nicht nur für den örtlichen Gebrauch, sondern auch für den Export in andere Teile Indonesiens, vor allem nach Sumatra. Ein Großteil der örtlichen Batikproduktion lag in den Händen der chinesischen Einwohner.

Das „Erkennungsmuster" der Batiken aus Lasem war ein blühender Baum auf einem ungemusterten, cremefarbenen Grund. Als Inspirationsquelle dienten zweifellos die indischen „Chintz"-Textilien von der Koromandel-Küste, die häufig den Lebensbaum darstellen, eines der gebräuchlichsten Motive in der asiatischen Kunst. Bis Ende des 18. Jahrhunderts wurden hunderttausende indischer Chintzstoffe nach Europa exportiert und einige auch in den indonesischen Archipel. Warum und wann die chinesischen Werkstätten in Lasem mit der Produktion örtlicher Varianten des Chintzmusters begannen, ist nicht bekannt. Man vermutet jedoch, dass dies in der ersten Hälfte des 19. Jahrhunderts geschah, als der Import von Textilien von der Koromandelküste zu Ende ging. Auf jeden Fall ist die Ähnlichkeit der Batiken aus Lasem, landläufig *kain laseman* genannt, mit den indischen Prototypen unverkennbar. Manche dieser Stoffe tragen einen vollständigen Lebensbaum, der gelegentlich aus einem Felsvorsprung hervorwächst (Tf. 23, 25, 29, 34). Öfter aber zeigt das Motiv blühende Zweige inmitten von Vögeln, Insekten und Schmetterlingen in Kombination mit Blütenranken. Phönixe und andere Fantasievögel geben diesem im Wesentlichen indischen Thema einen deutlich chinesischen Charakter (Tf. 26, 33, 34).

Batiken aus Lasem trugen oft auch figürliche Kompositionen wie z. B. chinesische und europäische Tiere (Tf. 28, 36) oder Neuheiten wie neuartige Verkehrsmittel: Fahrräder, Autos und Flugzeuge (Tf. 38). Gelegentlich findet man eine dekorativ stilisierte Inschrift, wie „SLAMET NJANG PAKE" – „Glück / Segen der Trägerin / dem Besitzer" (Tf. 37). Chinesinnen wie auch Javanerinnen von der Nordküste Javas trugen früher die erlesenen *laseman*-Röcke.

Technisch gesehen ist *laseman* eines der schwierigsten Batikmuster. Es handelt sich hier um die Technik des *latar putih* („weißer Hintergrund"), wobei farbige Motive auf einem weißen, ungefärbten Grund erscheinen. Dies bedeutete, dass die gesamte Hintergrundfläche mit einer dicken Wachsschicht abgedeckt werden musste und nur die Stellen, die später als rote oder blaue Figuren erscheinen sollten, offen bleiben durften, um die Farbe aufzunehmen. Man erreichte dies durch ein höchst akribisches Verfahren, das viel Geschicklichkeit und Geduld verlangte.
Ein weiteres charakteristisches Merkmal der Batiken aus Lasem sind die Farben. Der Hintergrund

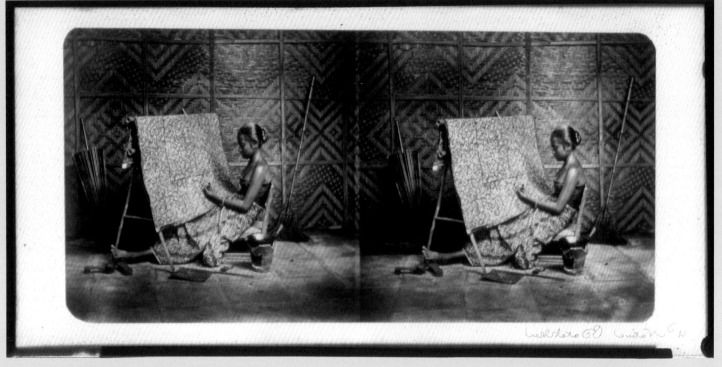

Die vermutlich erste Aufnahme
einer javanischen Frau bei der
Batikarbeit.
Stereo-Daguerrotypie,
W.B. Woodbury, 1858

Woman batiking, probably
the first batik photo ever.
Stereo glass plate by
W.B. Woodbury, 1858

dieser Stoffe ist nicht weiß, sondern cremefarben – erreicht durch starkes Einölen des Stoffes – und die berühmte rote Farbe (aus dem *mengkudu*-Farbstoff) ist vermutlich aufgrund der chemischen Zusammensetzung des dortigen Wassers besonders satt und intensiv.

In diesem Teil Javas werden Batikstoffe normalerweise nicht nach ihren Motiven benannt, sondern nach der Farbkombination. Eine Gemeinsamkeit fast aller in Nordjava produzierten Batiken ist die rote Farbe, genannt *bang*. Ausschließlich mit roter Farbe gefärbte Stoffe heißen *bang-bangan*. Da Rot als Fruchtbarkeitssymbol galt, standen sie oft mit der Hochzeitsfeier in Verbindung – z. B. als Bettüberwürfe für frisch verheiratete Paare (Tf. 67, 68, 70). Batiken in Blau und Rot – die üblichste Farbkombination der *laseman*-Stoffe – nennt man *kain bangbiru*. Stoffe mit ausschließlich dunkelblauer oder schwarzer Färbung heißen *kain kelengan* und werden als Trauerkleidung getragen (Tf. 35).

Im Gegensatz zu javanischen Männern, die Batikröcke bevorzugten, trugen die chinesischen und europäischen Bewohner Javas gern Batikhosen (*celana*), weswegen die Werkstätten Nordjavas früher eine Reihe solcher Kleidungsstücke produzierten (Tf. 40 - 41).

Semarang, eine weitere Stadt an der Nordküste Javas mit einem großen chinesischen Bevölkerungs-

anteil, produzierte einst Batiken mit Blumenmustern, die oftmals den *kain laseman* ähneln. Beide Städte spezialisierten sich nicht nur auf die Produktion von Batikkleidung, sondern fertigten auch die verschiedensten Zeremonialtextilien für chinesische Auftraggeber. Die wohl gebräuchlichsten waren Altartücher für den Hausaltar, *tok wi* genannt. In China waren solche Stoffe normalerweise bestickt, auf Java wurden die gleichen Muster hingegen in Batiktechnik ausgeführt (Tf. 65). *Mui li* waren Behänge, die man über dem Hauseingang anbrachte, um das Haus vor negativen Kräften zu schützen (Tf. 66). Bettüberwürfe, *kain sprei* (Tf. 67-70), waren ebenfalls beliebt. Chinesische Zeremonialtücher zeigen häufiger als Batikkleidung die chinesischen Symbole für Glück, Wohlstand und ein langes Leben, darüber hinaus Sagengestalten oder Szenen aus chinesischen Legenden.

Gelegentlich fanden zentraljavanische Motive Eingang in die Ornamentierung der Batiken Nordjavas. Ein Beispiel ist das Patchwork-Motiv *tambal*, eines der Hauptmuster Zentraljavas, das in diesem Teil der Insel häufig auftritt. Der Katalog zeigt das prachtvolle Exemplar eines Batikrockes (jetzt im Besitz des Deutschen Textilmuseums Krefeld) mit diesem Muster von 1860 - 1870 aus Cirebon oder Semarang. Das uralte *tambal*-Muster – ursprünglich ein Symbol für Armut und Entbehrung – erreicht auf diesem opulenten Stoff eine neue Ebene der Vollendung: Die sehr sorgfältig ausgeführten Motive wurden durch Goldauftrag – *prada* – weiter verschönert (Tf. 39).

Batiken aus Pekalongan

Pekalongan gehörte früher ebenfalls zu den großen Batikzentren Nordjavas. Ihr kommerzieller Erfolg gründete sich auf den Unternehmergeist einer Gruppe von Frauen der „Indischen". Auf Java als Kinder javanisch-holländischer oder chinesisch-holländischer Eltern geboren und mit holländischen Einwohnern verheiratet, genossen sie größere soziale Freiheiten als javanische Frauen und waren in der Lage, ein eigenes Geschäft als Einkommensquelle einzurichten.

Gelegentlich zeigt die Ornamentierung der Batiken aus Pekalongan zwar den Einfluss der indischen Chintze, doch zu ihrem Markenzeichen wurden große, bunte Bouquets europäischer Blumen, die sich auf einem *sarong* normalerweise vier- bis fünfmal auf einem Grund mit dichten kleinen Füllmustern wiederholen (Tf. 46-48, 51-52). Die beliebtesten Blumen waren Rosen, Lilien, Iris, Tulpen, Margeriten und Stiefmütterchen. Sorgfältig arrangiert, waren diese Blumen mit großer Liebe zum Detail konventionell-realistisch ausgeführt und von bunten Vögeln und Schmetterlingen umschwirrt. Durch geschicktes Schattieren und Überfärben erzielte man lebhafte, farbenfrohe Bilder. Die Werkstatt-Besitzerinnen hatten oft ihre eigenen Geheimrezepte für die Naturfarben. In späteren Jahren waren sie die Ersten, die mit synthetischen Farbstoffen experimentierten.

Die Kunden der indo-europäischen Werkstätten hatten jedoch nicht nur eine Vorliebe für Blumen. Ein weiteres beliebtes Thema waren Märchen wie Aschenputtel, Schneewittchen oder Rotkäppchen (Tf. 44). Da die Werkstatt-Eigentümerinnen meist christlichen Glaubens waren, fanden manchmal auch religiöse Motive, am häufigsten Engel, Eingang in die Batik-Ornamentierung (Tf. 42 - 43). Ein weiteres populäres Thema waren Spiele wie Karten- oder Dominospiele, vielleicht ein Hinweis auf den Lieblingszeitvertreib der Besitzer der betreffenden Röcke (Tf. 45).

Als weitere Neuheit führten die „indischen" Unternehmerinnen eine Wachssignatur auf Batikarbeiten der besten Qualität ein. Diese Praxis macht es

möglich, die Objekte zu bestimmen, zu datieren und Veränderungen der örtlichen Mode genauer zu verfolgen als in anderen Teilen Javas. Frau B. Fißer (ca. 1825-1905) war die vermutlich erste indo-europäische Batikherstellerin in Pekalongan, die mit dem Signieren ihrer Batiken begann (Tf. 53). Eliza van Zuylen (1863-1947) gründete um 1890 ihr eigenes Batikunternehmen, und nach zwei Jahrzehnten Geschäftstätigkeit besaß sie die größte indo-europäische Batikwerkstatt auf Java, die bis zum Ende des Zweiten Weltkrieges bestand. Das Markenzeichen ihrer Batikarbeiten waren sehr feine Blumenbouquets, die in ganz Pekalongan ihresgleichen suchten (Tf. 46-48). Frau A. J. F. Jans (ca. 1850 - ca. 1920) war die einzige Eigentümerin einer Batikwerkstatt, deren Eltern beide Holländer waren. Auf Java geboren und aufgewachsen, war sie jedoch zweifellos fest in der „indischen" Kultur verwurzelt. *Sarongs* aus ihrer Werkstatt zeigen florale Muster, ganz ähnlich wie die von van Zuylen (Tf. 49-52). Lien Metzelaar (ca. 1855-1930) begann 1880 mit dem Betrieb einer Batikwerkstatt, als sie nach dem frühen Tod ihres Ehemannes ihr Einkommen aufbessern musste. Sie war als lokale „Trendsetterin" bekannt und führte bei den Batikmustern Pekalongans eine Reihe von Neuerungen ein (Tf. 44 - 45).[5]

Ein weiterer Produktionszweig der Werkstätten Pekalongans waren Dekorationsstoffe für indo-eurasische Häuser. Im Gegensatz zu chinesischen Dekorationsstoffen, die häufig religiöse Symbole zeigten, trugen die indo-europäischen jedoch rein dekorative Batikmuster. Sie fanden als Servietten, Wandbehänge, Sesselschoner und Tischdecken Verwendung (Tf. 59).

Die floralen Batiken aus Pekalongan hatten einen solchen kommerziellen Erfolg, dass im Jahr 1927 beinahe 1100 Batikwerkstätten in der Stadt und den umliegenden Dörfern in Betrieb waren und diese beinahe ein Drittel der Gesamtbatikproduktion Javas stellten. Die große Mehrzahl der Werkstätten war auf die Massenproduktion von Kopien berühmter Muster spezialisiert und arbeitete meist mit der *batik cap*- (Kupferstempel-)Technik.[6]

Mehrere hochklassige Batikwerkstätten in Pekalongan wurden von Chinesinnen betrieben. Um 1910 erlangten florale *sarongs* aus den „indischen" Werkstätten bei der chinesischen Bevölkerung Nordjavas Beliebtheit als Kleidungsstücke, vielleicht, weil diese Gruppe unter der holländischen Regierung einen sozialen Aufstieg erlebte. Chinesische Batikwerkstätten begannen mit der Fertigung von Stoffen mit dem berühmten Motiv des Blumenbouquets, doch wurde dieser Stil meist dem Geschmack der neuen Kundschaft angepasst: Die europäischen Blumenarrangements enthielten auch Pfingstrosen und Chrysanthemen, und die Farbskala veränderte sich in Richtung Pastelltöne. Ein gutes Beispiel dieser Produktion sind die Batiken von The Tie Siet, die ihr Geschäft von etwa 1920 bis in die Fünfziger Jahre führte (Tf. 57 - 58).

Batiken aus Kudus

Um die vorige Jahrhundertwende blühte die Batikindustrie in ganz Java, mehrere regionale Zentren entwickelten einen ausgeprägten eigenen Stil der Textilornamentierung. Eines dieser Zentren war Kudus, eine kleine Stadt in Nordjava, bekannt für ihre Rolle bei der Einführung des Islam auf der Insel sowie für das interessante Sortiment an Batikarbeiten, die dort vor dem Zweiten Weltkrieg produziert wurden. Für die dort gefertigten *kain* und *sarongs* bevorzugte man Blumenarrangements im Stil Pekalongans auf einem kunstvoll gearbeiteten, dicht mit winzigen Ziermustern gefüllten Grund, der einen Eindruck von „Horror Vacui" vermittelt (Tf. 60 - 62). Ein braunfarbiger Hintergrund war ein weiteres beliebtes Merkmal der Batiken aus Kudus. In den späten Zwanzigern und Dreißigern wurde ein neues Musterarrangement namens *pagi sore* („Vormittag und Nachmittag") populär, bei dem die Rockoberfläche diagonal in zwei Hälften mit jeweils anderer Musterung geteilt war. So konnte man den Rock auf zweierlei Art und Weise tragen, wobei jedesmal ein anderes Muster sichtbar war (Tf. 61 - 62). Die Komposition des *pagi sore* erreichte vor allem im Zweiten Weltkrieg große Beliebtheit, als Baumwollstoffe knapp und Batikhersteller gezwungen waren, ein Stück Stoff bestmöglich zu nutzen.

Batiken für Sumatra

Ab Ende des 19. Jahrhunderts war ein erheblicher Teil der auf Nordjava produzierten Batiktextilien zum Export auf andere Inseln des indonesischen Archipels und nach Übersee bestimmt. Eines der Hauptimportländer war Sumatra, wo die gläubige muslimische Bevölkerung Stoffarten von besonderer Größe und Musterung verlangte.

Ein speziell für Sumatra bestimmtes Tuch war beispielsweise der *kudhung*, ein wesentlich größerer Schal als der javanische *slendang*, mit dem fromme Frauen Schultern und Kopf bedeckten. Eine besondere Gruppe bildeten Stoffe mit Zitaten aus dem Koran und Anrufungen Allahs in arabischer Schrift, die so genannten *batik kaligrafi*. Da die Hersteller dieser Tücher oft kein Arabisch verstanden, ist die entsprechende Schrift zuweilen unleserlich und vermittelt lediglich eine allgemeine Botschaft muslimischer Frömmigkeit (Tf. 71 - 72). Cirebon war das wichtigste auf die Fertigung solcher Tücher spezialisierte Zentrum, doch aufgrund der großen Nachfrage im ausgehenden 19. Jahrhundert begann die Produktion ähnlicher Batiktücher auch in Jambi auf Sumatra. Manchmal lässt sich nur schwer sagen, ob eine bestimmte Batik aus Java oder Sumatra stammt.

Auch das Zentrum Lasem war auf den Export von Tüchern nach Sumatra spezialisiert, doch behielten die Exporttextilien ihre charakteristische, einheimische Farbpalette sowie ihre aus der chinesischen Ikonografie abgeleiteten Motive (Tf. 75).

Eine weitere beliebte Gruppe waren Batiken, deren Musterung die sogenannten *sembagi*-Stoffe imitierte – die bedruckten Stoffe der Koromandel–Küste, die noch im 19. Jahrhundert in großer Zahl nach Sumatra exportiert wurden. Die blau-rote Musterung dieser Stoffe besteht aus regelmäßig wiederholten, medaillonartigen Einheiten und wurde auf den Batiken Sumatras gewissenhaft reproduziert (Tf. 73 - 74).

Die Sammlung Rudolf G. Smend enthält beinahe ausschließlich Stoffe aus der Zeit von ca. 1870 bis 1930, als die javanische Batik ihren Höhepunkt erreichte und sich unzählige regionale Varianten dieser Technik entwickelt hatten, entsprechend der unterschiedlichsten Ansprüche der Käufer dieser Stoffe auf Java und anderen Teilen des indonesischen Archipels.

Seitdem war die javanische Batik zahlreichen Veränderungen unterworfen. Die Wirtschaftskrise von 1935 führte zur Schließung vieler Werkstätten. Durch soziale Veränderungen nach dem Rückzug der Holländer und der Entstehung der Republik Indonesien im Jahr 1945 verschwand die Nachfrage nach bestimmten Batikarten, z. B. der „indischen" und der meisten chinesischen Batiken. Gleichzeitig gab es Bestrebungen, einen nationalen Batikstil zu schaffen und diese Textilien als „indonesische Tracht" zu vermarkten. Der indonesische Modedesigner Iwan Tirta führte eine Luxusversion der Batik in die Haute Couture ein. Heute ist handgemalte *batik tulis* ein Luxustuch; es muss sich gegen die stetig steigende Produktion von Siebdruckstoffen und die industrielle Produktion von Stoffen mit Imitations-Batikmustern behaupten. Doch obwohl sich die javanische Batik in einer schwierigen Lage befindet, zeigt die Sammlung Rudolf G. Smend, dass diese Textilgruppe in den letzten dreißig Jahren zweifellos bei Sammlern und Kennern asiatischer Kunst aus Übersee große Anerkennung gefunden hat. Heute gilt die javanische Batik allgemein als eine der großartigsten Textiltraditionen der Welt.

Anmerkungen:

1 In der zweiten Hälfte des 19. Jahrhundert wurde ein Kupferstempel, *cap*, zum Aufbringen des Wachses auf die Stoffoberfläche eingeführt. Dieser verkürzte den Fertigungsprozess erheblich, doch beschränkte er gleichzeitig das kreative Potential der Batiktechnik. Da die Sammlung Rudolf G. Smend ausschließlich javanische Batiken mit handgezeichneter Wachsreservierung enthält, wird *batik cap* hier nicht erörtert.
2 Hardjonagoro „The place of batik in the history and philosophy of Javanese textiles: a personal view". In: M. Gittinger (Hrsg.), Indonesian Textiles. Irene Emery Roundtable on Museum Textiles 1979 Proceedings, Textile Museum. Washington D.C. 1980, S. 230.
3 Nach javanischem Glauben hat das Motiv Zauberkräfte und wurde im 17. Jahrhundert von Sultan Agung geschaffen, dem berühmtesten Herrscher der Mataram-Dynastie. Tatsächlich ist das Muster wesentlich älter und wurde von der Dongson-Kultur zusammen mit der Bronzemetallurgie nach Südostasien gebracht.
4 Alit Veldhuisen-Djajasoebrata, Weavings of Power and Might. The Glory of Java. Rotterdam 1988, S. 31.
5 Harmen C. Veldhuisen, Batik Belanda 1840-1940, Jakarta 1993; Rens Heringa, Harmen C. Velduisen, Fabric of Enchantment. Batik from the North Coast of Java. Los Angeles County Museum of Art, 1996.
6 P. de Kat Angelino, Battikrapport, deel 2: Midden-Java, Batavia, Landsdrukkerij 1930-31, S. 215.

Two young men wearing batik with kawung design.
Java, c. 1920

JAVANESE BATIK

The art of wax design

Maria Wrońska-Friend

The Indonesian island of Java is the home of batik textiles – exquisite fabrics decorated with the wax-resist technique which are commonly recognised as one of the major accomplishments of Oriental art.

Many years ago, when visiting Java, Rudolf G. Smend was captivated by the sublime beauty of these textiles as well as being amazed by the complex skills required to accomplish these fabrics. Today his collection, recognised as one of the most important groups of such textiles in the world, contains the best examples of batiks made in diverse workshops operating in several parts of Java at the turn of 19/20th centuries – at the time when Javanese batik reached its technical and artistic apogee. It is a valuable resource which allows one to fully appreciate Javanese textile art, at the same time providing an insight into the social life and aesthetic preferences of the producers and users of these textiles.

Batik in Javanese culture

When trying to comprehend and appreciate this group of textiles, it is important to remember that Javanese batik is a cultural phenomenon which has no counterpart in Western textile tradition. Outside Java, batik is most frequently recognised as a cloth of great beauty, to be worn, admired and collected, or as a tangible manifestation of highly developed manual skills and specialised technological knowledge, an outcome of centuries-long experiments with natural dyes. But although it is true that Javanese batik is all of that, it is also much more – it is a fabric which has been imbued with complex symbolic meanings and which functions as a visual manifestation of Javanese beliefs, ethics and social order; as such batik textiles have been recognised as one of the most eminent expressions of Javanese culture.

Due to the great significance of these textiles in the social and ceremonial life of Javanese people, as well as because of the mental concentration required to produce some of the most complex designs, batik in Central Java is recognised not as a craft or a manual task, but as a discipline of the most refined arts, known as "halus". Batik shares this high position with gamelan music, the *wayang* shadow theatre as well as Javanese drama and poetry. Interestingly for Europeans, "high" Javanese culture does not encompass any of the disciplines of fine arts, such as sculpture or painting, which in the Western tradition have been commonly recognised as the most important medium of artistic expression. Instead on Java – and, indeed, throughout the whole of the Indonesian Archipelago – it is the textile art which has became the dominant discipline of visual arts and the major form through which the creative skills of these people have been expressed.

At another level of appreciation, the diverse iconography of batik textiles functions as a visual record, which mirrors the complex history of Java and an intense cultural exchange with nearby countries. Indonesia is situated at the cross-roads between the two major civilisations of Asia: India and China, and at least for the last two thousand years envoys, traders and representatives of governments of both powers maintained regular contacts with the Islands. A particularly strong cultural influence was exercised by the Indian Peninsula. It was manifested through the introduction to Java of the religious and artistic traditions of Buddhism and Hinduism, numerous trade goods – among which most prominently featured silk and cotton textiles, as well as script and literature – for example the Sanskrit epics of Ramayana and Mahabharata which have become a source of philosophical and ethical foundations for Javanese society. Also important were trade contacts with the Near East, which in the 16th century eventuated in the introduction of Islam to Java – a religion which until today remains the dominant faith of the island. At the same time, spices and other goods of the Indonesian Archipelago started to attract the attention of several European countries from which the Netherlands emerged as the colonial power and, until 1945, exercised its political control over the Archipelago.

Young girl, probably a njahi or concubine. Semarang, c. 1919

This complex mosaic of cultural traditions is reflected in the multitude of designs appearing on Javanese textiles. The surface of numerous batiks gives testimony to the creative skills in which ancient local traditions have been harmoniously combined with decorative principles and designs borrowed from Indian, Chinese, Arab and European art, creating a powerful cultural fusion which until today remains a trademark of Javanese culture.

Over the centuries, batik on Java has developed into a multitude of regional styles. Different types of batik textiles used to be worn by the Javanese and Sundanese, by Arab and Chinese residents on Java, by the racially mixed Indo-European population and by sultans and commoners. The multitude of colours and designs resulted in the creation of a rich visual language, in which the batik garment functioned as an expression of the ethnic and regional identity of the person wearing it, as well as an indicator of the social position, age and even marriage status. Until today batik textiles are used as important ceremonial and ritual attributes, frequently featuring in life-cycle ceremonies such as weddings, circumcision or pregnancy, during rituals at the sultan's court and as offerings to the Goddess of the South Seas – Ratu Kidul.

The origins

The Javanese term "batik", which became widely accepted in the majority of Western languages, signifies both the process of decorating textiles as well as the completed fabric. Batik is a complex and arduous technique of textile decoration in which hot, liquid wax is applied to those areas of the fabric which are to be protected during immersion in a dye-bath. As the layer of wax hardens on the surface of the cloth, it will "resist" the dye – and therefore the batik method is classified as one of the many techniques of resist-dyeing (others, for example, are ikat and tie-dye).

Surface dyeing with the use of liquid substances comes in various forms and has been practised in several parts of the world, in ancient as well as modern times. Usually either India or ancient Egypt has been identified as the original place of invention of this method, although it is also possible that dyeing with liquid resists was invented independently in several parts of the world. The Indian Peninsula is sometimes indicated as the area from which the batik technique was introduced into Java, yet closer examination of the tools and dyeing technology used in both regions points more frequently to differences than similarities.

The word "batik" appears for the first time in European as well as Javanese written sources quite late – only in the 17th century. The hot, humid climate of the Indonesian islands has allowed only on quite rare occasions the preservation of textiles for more than two or three centuries and therefore there are no ancient examples of Javanese textiles that have survived to our days. The theory that batik was developed on Java and at a relatively late date is supported by the fact that the technique of wax resist-dyeing is not known on Bali – an island which until the end of 15th century, prior to the advent of Islam, formed part of the Javanese-ruled Majapahit kingdom, and which until today continues the traditions of the Indian culture which dominated in this part of the Archipelago for more than a millennium. It is probable therefore that wax-resist dyeing on Java was developed relatively late – only in the 16th century, perhaps evolving from the simple technique of drawing direct designs on textiles.

Drawing the wax designs

Probably the most distinguished feature of Javanese batik textiles are the well defined, precise designs drawn with melted wax using a small copper tool, known as a *canting*. These tools come in various forms and sizes: there are *cantings* with a fine spout to draw the outline of the main designs, others with a much larger spout to apply a thick layer of wax to large areas which are to remain undyed, and others again with very fine spouts to place tiny dots of wax (usually fill-in patterns); dual spouts are used to draw parallel lines, etc.

The wax application is usually the task of women. The work is conducted in specialised workshops and is usually a team task. Each woman specialises in executing a different type of design: the most experienced person draws the initial outlines and is responsible for the extremely fine filling ornaments, while the less skilled one applies a thick coat of wax to large areas of the fabric, usually the background. The execution of more complex compositions requires the involvement of three to four specialist workers who can draw the full range of wax designs. The owner of the workshop is only in rare cases involved in wax application. His or her duties are to decide the composition of the cloth and the particular designs to be used, as well as to supervise and coordinate the work of the team. Until today, in many workshops, the most expensive batiks are usually made to the order of a customer.

In monochrome batik (which is only occasionally executed on Java), the cloth is covered just once with wax designs and dyed in one colour (pl. 35). Following the dye-bath, the wax is removed by immersion in boiling water, revealing a lighter design on a darker, dyed background. In cases of multicoloured batiks, the wax has to be applied as many times as there are colours – each time covering different parts of the fabric. As it is impossible to rectify any mistakes, the production of multicoloured batiks requires a lot of experience and advance planning.

Due to the fact that wax-resist is applied on Java by hand, each of the batik fabrics becomes a unique creation: two textiles decorated with the same designs may be similar, but they will never be the same.[1]

One of the most characteristic features of Javanese batik is the strong control and discipline applied to drawing the designs. Nothing is left to chance and improvisation is certainly not encouraged; the final product should reflect as closely as possible the initial intention of the producer of the fabric. Sometimes however, during the dyeing process, the layer of wax may crack, allowing the dye to penetrate the cloth and result in an irregular veining pattern. This random effect, so frequently utilised by European artists and recognised as a characteristic feature of this technique, is on Java frequently treated as a technical mistake and avoided. In particular, the cracking of wax during indigo dyeing is regarded as a major technical error which disqualifies the fabric.

The dyeing process

The use of wax as a resist substance means that the dyeing process may take place only in a cold or lukewarm dye-bath. This limitation greatly restricts the range of natural dyes which can be used in making batik textiles. In principle, there were only three natural dyes which, in the past, were commonly used on Java: *indigo*, *soga* (brown) and *mengkudu* (red). Although this range of colours may seem to be very limited, the Javanese batik producers and local dyers became most adept at overcoming this obstacle. Variations to recipes and the length of the dyeing process produced an extensive range of hues and shades, while skilled over-dyeing resulted in an increased range of colours.

Indigo (*nilo*) is probably the oldest and the most commonly used dye on Java. It is an oxidising dye, which requires complex processing with little tolerance for error. To obtain good quality colour, the fabric has to be immersed in the dyeing vat up to sixty times, and the whole process may take up to two weeks.

Brown colour (*soga*) is a tannin dye, made from an extract of three types of wood and bark. Soga dyeing is traditionally associated with Central Java, especially with the court cities of Yogyakarta and Surakarta, where even today, some of the batik workshops use natural *indigo* and *soga*.

The deep, red colour (*mengkudu*) which features so prominently in many batiks produced at the turn of 19/20th centuries on the north coast of Java (pls. 23-31, 50, 51, 53, 56), was occasionally used until mid-20th century. This is an alizarin dye, extracted from the roots of a small tree (*morinda citrifolia*). Similar to *soga*, *mengkudu* is a mordant dye and requires a complex pre-treatment of the fabric. The dyeing process itself was also tedious and time consuming – the dye had to be rubbed into the cloth at least once a day for more than three weeks.

The use of natural dyes required complex technological knowledge, obtained through years of practice and experiments. The dyeing formulas were only rarely written and were usually transmitted orally or learned through practice; in some cases they were known only to the owner of the workshop and were lost with that person's death.

Synthetic dyes, which started to appear on Java from the end of 19th century and which nowadays are commonly used, require less specialised knowledge and equipment. They have significantly reduced the amount of time required to dye the cloth, but have introduced much greater uniformity to the colours of Javanese batiks, levelling regional differences.

The time required to make a batik cloth depends upon a range of factors, the main ones being the complexity of the design, the number of colours used as well as whether natural or chemical dyes are applied. It may take four to eight weeks to make a two-colour skirt of medium quality using synthetic dyes, but in the case of the highest quality batiks, like many of those which feature in Rudolf G. Smend's collection, the time required would be six to eight months of daily work.

Batik as a Javanese garment

Batik textiles were most frequently used as apparel – skirts, breast-cloths, sashes, baby carriers and headscarves. Only in rare cases was the technique applied to the production of decorative textiles. Such fabrics were usually made for the Chinese and Indo-European community (pls. 59, 63-70).

Traditional Javanese garments do not require any tailoring. They are constructed from rectangular or square pieces of fabric, the size of which and the way they are wrapped determining their function. Most frequently the batik technique is applied to produce two types of skirts: *kain panjang* and *sarong*.

The so called "long-skirt" – *kain panjang* is made of a single piece of fabric which is approximately 1,10 m wide and 2,5 m long. The skirt is uniformly covered with repetitive units of the pattern (pls. 1-11) and is worn tightly wrapped around the hips. *Kain panjang* is the official dress of the Javanese aristocracy, and in most cases there is no gender differentiation: the same patterns can be worn by men and women.

Sarong, a tubular skirt with both ends sewn together, could be called a "short skirt", because it requires just over two meters of batiked cloth. It is worn as informal dress in Central Java and has become a popular garment in other parts of the island. The *sarong* is usually decorated with a distinctive front field known as *kepala* ("head") which initially used to feature two rows of opposing triangles known as *tumpal* design (pls. 24, 29, 31, 37). At a later date, especially in batiks created on the north coast of Java, the triangles were frequently replaced with floral arrangements (pls. 21, 22, 30, 43-54).

Although nowadays Javanese women complement a batiked skirt with a tailored blouse *kebaya*, in the past and even today at the Central-Javanese courts, they wear a long rectangular fabric, tightly tied around the torso and known as *kemben* (pls. 13-17). A batik sash, known as *selendang* would complement the female costume (pl. 23). For Javanese aristocrats the formal dress was complemented by a square head-cloth *iket kepala* (pl. 12).

Batik costume functions not only as an utilitarian garment, be it everyday or ceremonial, but also acts as a symbolic manifestation of the unity of the opposing forces of the universe. According to ancient Javanese beliefs, the universe is composed of antithetical forces, which, similar to the Chinese ying and yang system, oppose but also complement each other. Batik textiles, being soft and pliable and made chiefly by women, stand for the female element; the male aspect of the universe is exemplified by the daggers *kris* and other types of weapons – objects which are hard, pointed and made by men. In the official court dress of Central Java, a batik skirt and *kris* dagger are always worn together, thus complementing each other and symbolically representing the totality of the universe. The garment thus becomes the ultimate expression of cosmic balance, in which antithetical forces, expressed through their material form of a cloth and a weapon, have been unified.

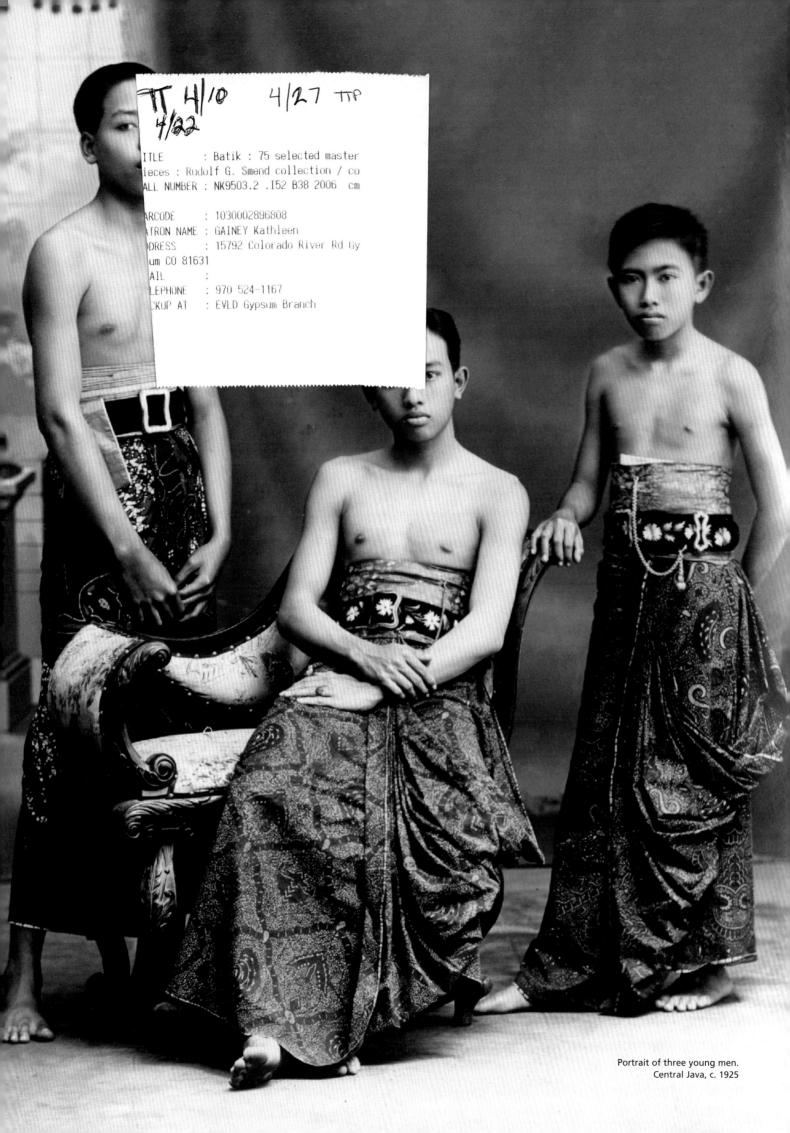

Portrait of three young men.
Central Java, c. 1925

Batiks of Central Java

The art of the Central Javanese batik has been strongly associated with the traditions of the two local courts of the sultans of Surakarta and Yogyakarta, institutions which until today have exercised profound influence on the political and cultural life of the area.

The sultans have always acted as patrons of local arts, and although today batiks are no longer made at the courts, in the past the waxing of textiles used to be an important occupation of the ladies-in-waiting. Today to some extent, this tradition is still continued by the wives of Javanese aristocrats. The drawing of controlled, precise wax designs has become an exercise in developing personal skills such as patience, concentration and precision. It was also a way of meditating, the aim of which was "to calm the disturbed soul" [2]. Consequently, batik achieved the status of one of the most important arts, with each of the courts developing a distinctive range of colours and designs. The collection of Rudolf G. Smend contains a group of textiles associated with the palace of Yogyakarta, which provides an excellent insight into the traditions of Javanese court batik (pls. 1-3, 7, 8, 10, 12, 13-19).

Central-Javanese batik textiles, usually representing the blue and brown range of colours, are known as *kain sogan* (from the brown dye *soga*). At the court of Yogyakarta these two colours appear on a white, crisp background resulting in clearly outlined, contrasting designs (pls.1-4), while the court of Surakarta opted for much softer, yellowish hues (pl. 5).

Some of the batik designs are believed to have special powers, and at the end of the 18th century both the courts at Surakarta and Yogyakarta issued edicts restricting their use to the sultan and high court officials. These rules are even today observed within the courts and the use of a particular design signifies the social position of the wearer. The group of "forbidden" (*larangan*) designs includes the visually stunning *parang rusak* ("broken dagger") motif, composed of continuous, wavy bands which run in diagonal rows across the whole surface

High ranking Javanese lady. Central Java, c. 1920

of the cloth (pls. 1, 8). This distinctive, ancient design has been restricted at both courts to the exclusive use of the sultan and his immediate family.[3]

Sawat is another design from the larangan group. It has probably evolved from the palmette design, one of the most popular decorative motifs appearing in the art of the Near East and South Asia. On Java it is interpreted as a symbolic representation of Garuda, the mythical bird, which used to carry the god Vishnu – a popular deity of the Hindu-Javanese pantheon (pls. 1 - 2). Another design which was most probably introduced through trade cloths is lar – a tear-drop motif, in India known as buta, which features prominently in the decoration of Kashmiri shawls. On Java this design represents a single wing of the Garuda bird and was destined for persons of lower rank at Javanese courts (pls. 12 - 13).

Kawung, an ancient four-petal flower design, which is already known from the Indus valley civilisations (Mohenjo-Daro and Harappa, approximately 2500 BC), appears frequently on Java, decorating garments of stone statues representing Hindu gods and the deified rulers. At the Yogyakarta court kawung has been classified as a larangan design and frequently appears on batiks, either as the main motif or in combination with other designs (pl. 2 and photo p. 43).

Another favourite motif decorating Central Javanese fabrics is tambal – an assemblage of batik designs which imitate patchwork cloth (pls. 4-7). This is another design which has a rich cultural history associated with the religious traditions of Asia. Patched robes frequently feature as a dress worn by Buddha and his disciples, being an expression of poverty vows and advocacy of an austere life. In Islam the followers of the Sufi order used to wear ragged, patched garments to signify their contempt for worldly goods. A similar dress, the patchwork jacket Kyahi Antakusuma ("the venerable many-flowered") was an heirloom robe at the Yogyakarta court and worn by the sultan during the most important ceremonies, such as Garebeg[4]. Considered by Javanese people to have healing and protective powers, especially to ward off sickness and evil, tambal became one of the most significant batik designs on Java.

Textiles with printed and woven designs were for centuries traded from India and made a strong impact on the decorative style of Indonesian fabrics. The most important of all the trade textiles, recognised as the most luxurious of all Indian fabrics, was patola – a silk cloth decorated with the extremely complex technique of double ikat. Due to technical limitations, patola designs do not feature continuous lines but are built of tiny, square, drop-like units. In Javanese batik these distinctive patterns have been translated into the nitik design (pls. 6-8). The execution of this design in wax is certainly the ultimate test in patience and diligence, and requires the use of a specially constructed canting.

The majority of batik designs associated with the Central-Javanese courts feature floral forms in abstract geometrical stylisation. It is possible that this decoration reflects the influence of Islamic art. Although small animal figures feature in some of these batiks, human figures are absent. The only referral to human beings occurs through the medium of the wayang figures – shadow theatre puppets (pls. 9-11). On Java excerpts from the Indian epics Mahabharata or Ramayana are the favourite repertoire of the shadow theatre, performed to mark important events and celebrations. On batik textiles, the wayang design was given the name ciptoning, and as wayang figures represent wisdom and experience, it appears on skirts worn by older and well respected persons when attending events like weddings or court ceremonies. For very special occasions, batik cloth may be covered with gold leaf – prada (pl. 11).

Batik skirts of the *kain panjang* type are worn as the official garment at court and by Javanese aristocracy. On very special occasions, such as a coronation or the Garebeg ceremony, the sultan wears a *dodot* – a ceremonial skirt, which is almost four times as large as *kain panjang*. The cloth is wrapped around the body, usually with one end forming a long train, or with a fold hanging on one side. The central field of *dodot* which is rectangular or in the shape of a diamond, remains undyed and only the sides are decorated with important designs, such as *parang rusak* or *semen* – a stylised rendition of the sacred landscape. Although *dodot* is strongly associated with royal ceremonies, it may be worn by brides and bridegrooms on their wedding day. According to Javanese tradition, the newly wed couple, even if they are of common descent, become "queen and king" for the day of their marriage and the use of the royal garment confirms this special status (pls. 18 - 19).

A quite distinctive visual language governs the use of breast-cloths *kemben*, which until today remain a part of official female dress at the Central-Javanese courts. Unmarried women wear *kemben* of the *byur* type, which is uniformly covered with a decorative design (pl. 13). *Kemben* for married women carries a dramatic, diamond-like field (*sidangan*) which acts as a visual symbol of their wedded status (pls. 14 - 17). The field is frequently lined with very fine green, blue or purple silk. The colours are not a matter of personal preference but indicative of a situation or ceremony in which *kemben* is used. For example, black and white *kemben* (known as *bangun tulak*; pl. 17) is used as a protective cloth in most vulnerable moments of life such as pregnancy or sickness, while green and white breast-cloths are offered to Ratu Kidul – the Goddess of South Seas and spiritual consort of Javanese sultans.

In some *kemben* the technique of batik has been combined with other types of resist dyeing such as *plangi* (tie-dye) and tritik (stitch-dyeing). Multi-coloured fabrics of this kind are known as *kain kembangan* ("flowered cloths") and are the most interesting examples of women's dress on Java (pl. 16).

Sarong – a tubular skirt, is worn in Central Java only as casual dress, but even these fabrics sometimes feature interesting examples of batik designs (pls. 20 - 22). The range of decorative motifs is sometimes similar to those which appear on more formal garments like *kain panjang*, but their arrangement is organised in a free manner, not being restrained by the rules of palace protocol. For example, the *kawung* design, associated with the sultan's court, is interspaced with rows of birds and floral tendrils (pl. 22), while the *sawat* design, placed on the background of freely drawn floral arrangements with the front section of the cloth featuring baskets of flowers, testifies to the influence of European iconography (pl. 21).

North Coast

A distinctive batik tradition has developed in the towns situated in the northern part of Java, in the area known as *pasisir*. Local coastal towns have for centuries been involved in the maritime trade and have developed strong commercial links with the countries of the Near East, India and China. The manifold iconography of local textiles reflects the ethnic and cultural diversity of this area, where large groups of Arabs, Chinese and Indian settlers have, for centuries, being coexisting with the Javanese and Sundanese population. Another group with a distinctive identity were the "Indische" – mixed Indo-Eurasian population, descendants of Dutch, Javanese or Chinese parents, born and brought up on Java.

Unlike Central Java, where the batik designs used to reflect the social position of a person, textiles produced on North Java stressed the ethnic identity of the wearer. The major centres of batik production were Pekalongan, Cirebon, Semarang, Lasem, Kudus, Juana and Demak. Many of the batik workshops used to be run by non-Javanese entrepreneurs – women from the "Indische" group, Chinese residents who on Java are known as *Peranakan*, as well as Arab migrants from Yemen.

Batiks from Lasem

At the end of 19th century, Lasem was one of the largest batik centres in this part of Java, producing fabrics for local consumption as well as for export to other parts of Indonesia, especially Sumatra. A large portion of the local batik production was in the hands of Chinese residents.

The "signature" design of Lasem batiks was a blossoming tree, placed on a plain, creamy, background. There is no doubt that the inspiration came from the Indian "chintz" textiles produced on the Coromandel Coast, fabrics which frequently feature the tree of life – one of the most pervasive designs in Asian art. Until the end of 18th century, hundreds of thousands of Indian chintz cloths used to be exported to Europe and, some of them, to the Indonesian Archipelago. We do not know why and when the Chinese workshops at Lasem started to produce the local renderings of the chintz design – one may presume only that this may have happened in the first half of 19th century, at the time when the import of textiles from the Coromandel Coast came to an end. In any case, the similarity of the batiks produced at Lasem, commonly known as *kain laseman*, to their Indian prototype is unmistakable. On some of these fabrics we find the complete image of the tree of life which occasionally grows out from a rocky outcrop (pls. 23, 25, 29, 34), but more frequently the design features blossoming branches, surrounded by birds, insects and butterflies, combined with floral tendrils. Phoenixes and other fantastic birds give this primarily Indian theme a distinctive Chinese character (pls. 26, 33 - 34).

Batiks from Lasem also frequently featured figurative compositions, for example Chinese and European animals (pls. 28, 36) or novelty items, such as new means of travel: bicycles, cars and aeroplanes (pl. 38). Occasionally one finds a decoratively stylised inscription, such as "SLAMET NJANG PAKE" – "Luck / blessing for the owner / wearer" (pl. 37).

The exquisite laseman skirts used to be worn by Chinese as well as Javanese-European ("Indische") women from the north coast of Java.

In technical terms, laseman is one of the most difficult batik designs. It represents the *latar putih* ("white background") technique, in which coloured designs appear on a light, undyed background. It means that a thick layer of wax had to cover all of the background area, leaving open for dye penetration only these places which would later appear as red or blue figures. This is an extremely painstaking technique, requiring much skill and patience.

Another characteristic feature of Lasem batiks are their colours. The background of these fabrics is not white but creamy – the result of heavy oiling of the cloth, while the famous red colour (achieved with *mengkudu* dye) is very deep and intense, probably due to the chemical composition of the local water.

In this part of Java batik fabrics are usually named not after their designs but their colour combination. The unifying feature of almost all batiks produced on North Java is the red colour, known as *bang*. Fabrics dyed with just the red colour are known as *bang-bangan* and as red was the symbol of fertility, they were frequently associated with the wedding ceremony – for example, used as bed covers for newly wed couples (pls. 67 - 68, 70). Batiks featuring blue and red – the most common colour combination of laseman fabrics – are known as *kain bang-biru*. Fabrics which have been dyed with only dark blue or black are called *kain kelengan* and worn as mourning dresses (pl. 35).

Unlike Javanese men who favour batik skirts, Chinese and European residents on Java enjoyed wearing batik trousers (*celana*) and a range of such garments used to be produced in the workshops of North Java (pls. 40 - 41).

Semarang, another coastal town on the north coast of Java with a large Chinese population, used to produce batiks with floral designs which in many cases resemble *kain laseman*. Both towns specialised not only in the production of batiked garments but also used to produce a diverse range of ceremonial cloths for Chinese clients. Probably most common were the covers for home altars, known as *tok wi*. In China such fabrics would usually be embroidered, but on Java the same designs were executed in the batik technique (pl. 65). *Mui li* were hangings, placed above the entrance to the house, with the aim of protecting it from negative forces (pl. 66). Bed covers were also popular, known as *kain sprei* (pls. 67 - 70). Chinese ceremonial cloths, more frequently than batiked garments feature the Chinese symbols of luck, prosperity and long life, mythical characters as well as scenes from Chinese legends.

TAN-TJIE-LAN
BATAVIA

On some occasions, the designs of Central Java entered the decoration of batiks produced on North Java. For example *tambal* – the patchwork motif, one of the most prominent Central-Javanese designs, can frequently be found in this part of the island. This book shows a splendid example of a batik skirt (now in the possession of the Deutsches Textilmuseum Krefeld) with this design, which was produced between 1860-1870 in Cirebon or Semarang. The ancient *tambal* design – originally a symbol of poverty and austerity, has been brought on this luxurious fabric to new levels of excellence: the most carefully executed designs have been further enhanced with the application of gold leaf *prada* (pl. 39).

Batiks from Pekalongan

Pekalongan used to be another major batik centre of North Java. Its commercial success was due to the entrepreneurial spirit of a group of mixed-raced "Indische" women. Born on Java from mixed Javanese-Dutch or Chinese-Dutch parents and married to Dutch residents, they enjoyed greater social freedom than Javanese women and were able to set up their own income-producing businesses.

Although, occasionally, the decoration of Pekalongan batiks also testifies to the influence of Indian chintz, the trademark design of these fabrics became large, colourful bouquets of European flowers, usually repeated four or five times on the surface of a *sarong* and set on a background densely covered with small fill-in designs (pls. 46 - 48, 51 - 52). Roses, lilies, irises, tulips, daisies and pansies were the favourite flowers. The carefully arranged flowers, around which buzzed small colourful birds and butterflies, were executed in a realistic convention, with great care for detail. Skilful shading and over-dyeing resulted in vibrant, colourful images. The owners of these workshops frequently had their own secret formulas for natural dyes and in later years were the first ones to experiment with synthetic dyes.

However, the clients of Indo-European workshops favoured not only flowers. Another favourite theme was fairy-tales, such as Cinderella, Snow White or Red Riding Hood (pl. 44). As the owners of these workshops were usually Christians, sometimes also religious motifs, most frequently angels, entered the batik decoration (pls. 42 - 43). Another popular theme was games, such as cards or dominoes – perhaps being a reference to the favourite past-time of the owners of these skirts (pl. 45).

Another novelty introduced by the Indische entrepreneurs was to place a wax signature on the best quality batiks. This practice permits us to identify and date the batiks, as well as follow changes in local fashion to a greater degree than is possible in other parts of Java. Mrs B. Fißer (c. 1825-1905) was probably the first Indo-European batik producer in Pekalongan who started to sign her batiks (pl. 53). Eliza van Zuylen (1863-1947) who around 1890 started her own batik business, after two decades of operations owned the largest Indo-European batik workshop on Java, which existed until end of the Second World War. The trademark of her batiks was extremely fine bouquets of flowers, unequaled in all of Pekalongan (pls. 46 - 48). Mrs A. J. F. Jans (c. 1850 - c. 1920) was the only owner of a batik workshop in Pekalongan whose parents were both Dutch. However, born and brought up on Java, she was certainly well entrenched in the "Indische" culture. *Sarongs* from her workshop represent floral designs, quite similar to ones made by van Zuylen (pls. 49-52). Lien Metzelaar (c. 1855-1930) started to operate a batik workshop in 1880, when she had to supplement her income following the early death of her husband. She was recognised as a local "trendsetter" and introduced a number of innovations to the designs of Pekalongan batiks (pls. 44 - 45).[5]

Another production line of Pekalongan workshops was decorative fabrics for Indo-Eurasian homes. However, unlike the Chinese decorative cloths which frequently featured religious symbols, the Indo-European ones were batiked with purely ornamental designs. They were used as serviettes, wall-hangings, anti-makassars (armchair covers) and tablecloths (pl. 59).

Two ladies, photo by Tan Tjie Lan.
Batavia, c. 1910

Mangku Nagoro VII of Surakarta and
his wife the Ratu Timur visiting
Gusti Bagus Djilantik of Karangasem
(left). Bali, c. 1920

The commercial success of the floral batiks of Pekalongan was so great that in 1927 there were close to 1100 batik workshops operating in the town and nearby villages, which constituted almost one-third of the total batik production on Java. The vast majority of the workshops specialised in the mass-production of copies of the famous designs, using the *batik cap* (copper stamp) technique.[6]

Several of the high quality batik workshops at Pekalongan were operated by Chinese. Around 1910, floral *sarongs* produced in the "Indische" workshops became the popular garment of the Chinese population of North Java, perhaps due to the social promotion of this group by the Dutch government. Chinese batik workshops commenced producing fabrics with the famous bouquet design, but usually the style was adjusted to suit the taste of new clients: the European floral arrangements included peonies and chrysanthemums, while the

colours changed into a more pastel range. Batiks produced by The Tie Siet, who managed his business from about 1920 until the 1950s, provide a good example of such production (pls. 57-58).

Batiks from Kudus

The turn of 19/20th centuries is the period of the blooming of the batik industry all over Java, with a number of regional centres developing a distinctive style of textile decoration. One of them was Kudus – a small town in North Java, well-known for the part it played in the introduction of Islam to the island, as well as for an interesting range of batiks which used to be produced here before the Second World War. Local *sarong* and *kain* favoured Pekalongan-style floral arrangements, placed on an intricate background, densely filled with tiny decorative motifs which create an impression of "horror vacui" (pls. 60-62). A brown-coloured background was another favourite feature of batiks made at Kudus. In the late 1920-1930s a new design arrangement became popular, known as *pagi sore* ("morning and afternoon"), in which the surface of the skirt was divided diagonally into two halves, each filled with a different design. In this way the same skirt could be worn in two ways, each time revealing different pattern (pls. 61 - 62). The *pagi sore* arrangement became very popular especially during the Second World War, when the shortage of cotton fabric pressed the batik producers to make the most of one piece of cloth.

Batik for Sumatra

From the end of 19th century, a significant part of batik textiles produced on North Java was destined for the other islands of the Indonesian Archipelago as well as overseas. One of the main importers was Sumatra, where the devoted Muslim population required special types of fabrics, both in respect of size as well as designs.

For example, a specifically Sumatran cloth was the *kudhung* – a scarf of much larger size than the Javanese *slendang* and used by pious women to cover their shoulders and heads. A special group were the so-called *batik kaligrafi* – fabrics decorated with quotes from the Koran and invocations of Allah in Arabic script. As in most cases the producers of these cloths were illiterate, the Arabic script is illegible, sending just a general message of Muslim piety (pls. 71 - 72). Although Cirebon was the main centre specialising in the production of this type of cloth, due to great demand at the end of 19th century, production of similar batik cloths started in Jambi on Sumatra. In some cases it is quite difficult to state whether a particular batik was made on Java or Sumatra.

Lasem was another centre specialising in exporting cloths to Sumatra, however the exported goods retained the characteristics of the local range of colours as well as designs derived from Chinese iconography (pl. 75).

Another group of popular textiles were batiks with designs imitating the so called *sembagi* fabrics – printed cloths from the Coromandel Coast, which used to be exported to Sumatra in large quantities even in the 19th century. The blue and red designs of these fabrics, composed of metrically repeated medallion-like units, were faithfully reproduced in Sumatran batiks (pls. 73 - 74).

The collection of Rudolf G. Smend contains almost exclusively fabrics from the period c. 1870-1930, from the days when Javanese batik reached its technical peak and when innumerable regional variations of this technique were developed, reflecting the complex needs of the consumers of these fabrics on Java and in other parts of the Indonesian Archipelago.

Since then Javanese batik has undergone numerous transformations. The economic crisis of 1935 resulted in the closure of many workshops. Social changes following the withdrawal of the Dutch and the creation of the Republic of Indonesia in 1945 meant that the market for certain types of batiks – like the "Indische" and most of the Chinese ones – ceased to exist. At the same time, attempts were undertaken to create a national style of batik and to promote these textiles as the "dress of Indonesia". Iwan Tirta, Indonesian fashion designer, introduced a luxurious version of batik into haute couture. Today, hand-drawn *batik tulis* is becoming a cloth of luxury; it has to compete with the ever-increasing production of silk-screen printing and industrial production of fabrics which imitate batik designs. Although on Java batik may find itself in a challenging situation, there is no doubt that, as Rudolf G. Smend's collection indicates, during the last thirty years this group of fabrics has gained major recognition among overseas collectors and connoisseurs of Asian art. Today, Javanese batik is universally recognised as one of the greatest textile traditions of the world.

Notes:

1 In the second half of the 19th century a copper stamp cap, was introduced to apply wax to the surface of the fabrics, significantly shortening the process of the production, but at the same time limiting the creative potential of the batik technique. As Rudolf G. Smend's collection contains only Javanese batiks decorated with hand-applied resist, *batik cap* will not be discussed here.
2 Hardjonagoro "The place of batik in the history and philosophy of Javanese textiles: a personal view". In: M. Gittinger (ed), Indonesian Textiles. Irene Emery Roundtable on Museum Textiles 1979 Proceedings, Textile Museum. Washington D. C. 1980, p. 230.
3 According to Javanese beliefs, the design has magical power and was created in the 17th century by Sultan Agung – the most famous ruler of the Mataram dynasty. In reality, this design is much older and was introduced to Southeast Asia with the Dongson culture, associated with bronze metallurgy.
4 Alit Veldhuisen-Djajasoebrata, Weavings of Power and Might. The Glory of Java. Rotterdam 1988, p. 31.
5 Harmen C. Veldhuisen, Batik Belanda 1840-1940, Jakarta 1993; Rens Heringa, Harmen C. Velduisen, Fabric of Enchantment. Batik from the North Coast of Java. Los Angeles County Museum of Art, 1996.
6 P. de Kat Angelino, Battikrapport, deel 2: Midden-Java, Batavia, Landsdrukkerij 1930-31, p. 215.

Street seller with movable food stall, photo attributed to A.S. Cohan. Yogyakarta, c. 1890

Kandjeng Ratu Madu Retno,
member of the family of
Sultan Hamengku Buwono VII
of Yogyakarta,
photo by K. Cephas.
Yogyakarta, c. 1885

DIE SAMMLUNG

THE COLLECTION

Zu den Abbildungsunterschriften:
Maße: Angaben Breite x Höhe
Material: Baumwolle (wenn nicht anders bezeichnet)

Note on the captions:
Measurements given as width x height
Material: cotton (unless otherwise stated)

Regent en Raden Ajoe
Toeloeng Agoeng.

1
Skirt *kain panjang*
Sultan's court (*kraton*)
at Yogyakarta
Central Java, 1930-1940
284 x 104 cm

Decorated with designs restricted to use by the Javanese
sultan and his family: diagonal pattern *parang rusak*
("broken dagger") and *sawat*
(symbolic representation of
the mythical bird Garuda).

Musterung mit Motiven, die
dem javanischen Sultan und
seiner Familie vorbehalten
waren: diagonal verlaufendes
parang rusak- („zerbrochener
Dolch-") Muster mit sawat
(symbolische Darstellung des
mythologischen Vogels
Garuda).

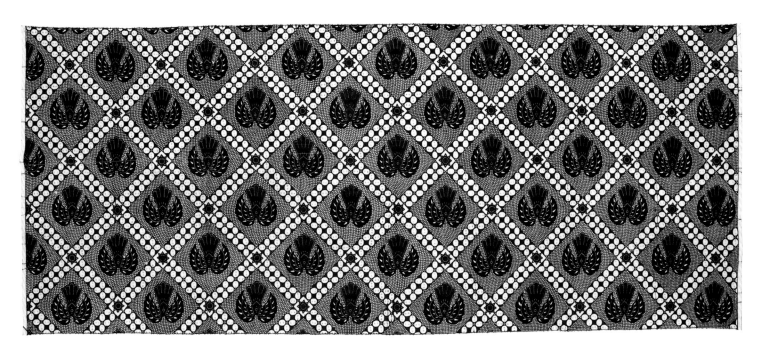

2
Skirt *kain panjang*
Sultan's court (*kraton*)
at Yogyakarta
Central Java, 1930-1935
250 x 103 cm

Decorated with designs restricted to use by the Javanese
sultan and his family: *sawat*
(symbolic representation of
the mythical bird Garuda) and
bands of the ancient *kawung*
design which divide the fields.

Musterung mit Motiven, die
dem javanischen Sultan und
seiner Familie vorbehalten
waren: sawat (symbolische
Darstellung des mythologi-
schen Vogels Garuda) und
Streifen des alten kawung-
Musters als Feldteiler.

Regent and Raden Aju
of Tulung Agung,
photo by Sie Sie Lin.
East Java, 1905

3
Skirt *kain panjang*
Sultan's court (*kraton*)
at Yogyakarta
Central Java, 1925-1930
259 x 104 cm

Design *prabu anom* ("second prince"), associated with the sultan's court.

Muster prabu anom (*„Zweiter Prinz"*), dem Hof des Sultans zugehörig.

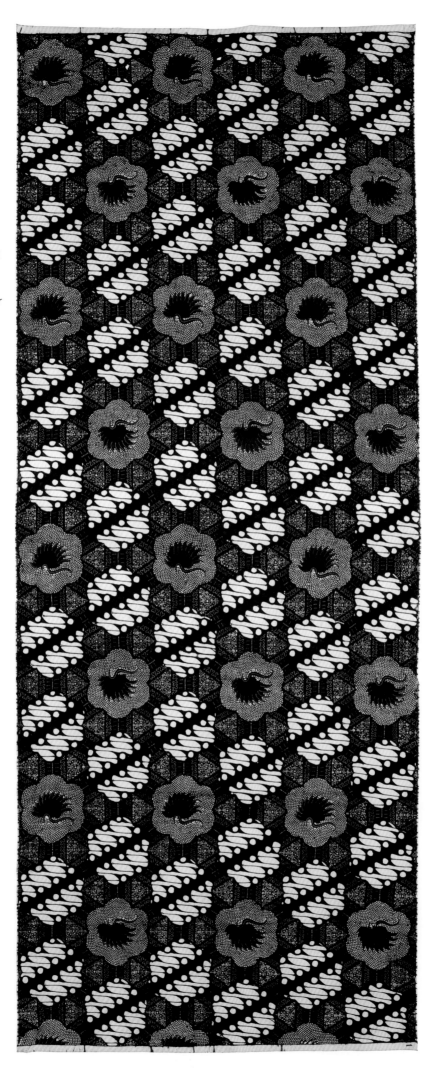

4
Skirt *kain panjang*
Yogyakarta
Central Java, 1935-1940
250 x 104 cm

Decorated with the *tambal*
("patchwork") design,
believed to have protective
powers.

Ornamentierung mit dem
tambal- *("Patchwork-")*
Muster, dem man schützende
Kräfte zuschreibt.

5
Skirt *kain panjang*
Surakarta
Central Java, 1930-1935
255 x 107 cm

The *tambal* ("patchwork")
pattern, composed of numerous small units of batik
designs, is believed to have
protective powers.

Dem tambal- *("Patchwork-")
Muster, das sich aus zahlreichen kleinen Batikmustern
zusammensetzt, werden
schützende Kräfte zugeschrie-
ben.*

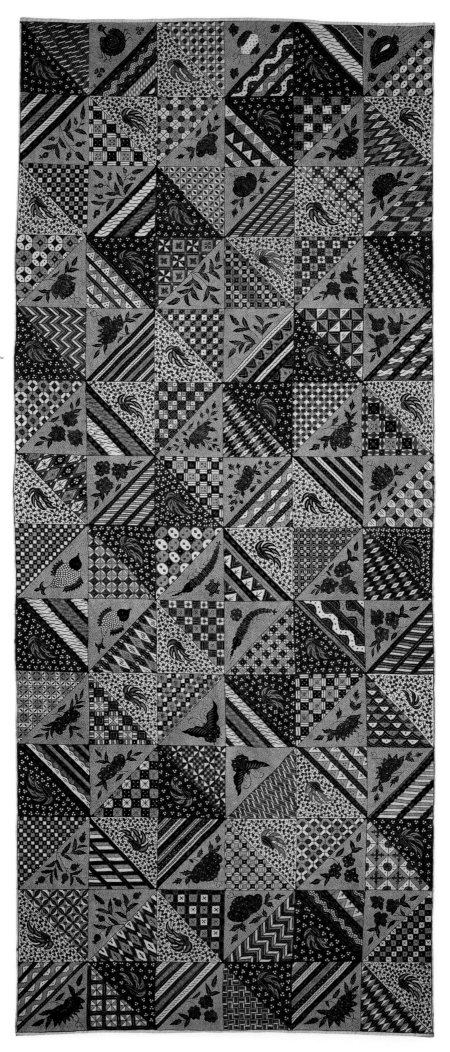

6
Skirt *kain panjang*
Yogyakarta
Central Java, 1930-1935
267 x 105 cm

The *tambal nitik* composition
represents an array of designs
associated with the highly
valued silk fabrics *patola*
which for centuries were
imported from India to Java.

Die tambal nitik-*Komposition*
zeigt eine Reihe von Mustern,
welche an die hoch geschätz-
ten patola-*Seidenstoffe erin-*
nern, die jahrhundertelang
von Indien nach Java einge-
führt wurden.

7
Skirt *kain panjang*
Sultan's court (*kraton*)
at Yogyakarta
Central Java, 1930 - 1935
245 x 103 cm

The *tambal nitik* composition
represents an array of designs
associated with the highly
valued silk fabrics *patola*
which for centuries were
imported from India to Java.

Die tambal nitik-*Komposition*
zeigt eine Reihe von Mustern
aus dem Zusammenhang der
hoch geschätzten patola-
Seidenstoffe, die jahrhunder-
telang von Indien nach Java
eingeführt wurden.

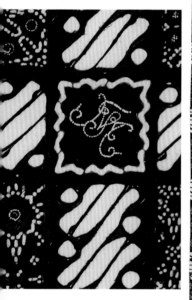

8
Skirt *kain panjang*
Sultan's court (*kraton*)
at Yogyakarta
Central Java, 1930-1935
245 x 105 cm

Motif *keong sari* ("pretty
snails") placed on a background filled with the *parang
rusak* ("broken dagger")
design.

Das Motiv keong sari *(„hüb-
sche Schnecken") auf einem
Hintergrund mit dem* parang
rusak *(„zerbrochener Dolch")
als Füllmuster.*

9
Skirt *kain panjang*
Yogyakarta
Central Java, 1935 - 1940
245 x 105 cm

The design *ciptoning* represents shadow theatre marionettes *(wayang)* placed on
the *dele kecer* design ("scat-
tered soy beans"). *Wayang*
figures indicate wisdom and
experience and therefore
skirts with such designs are
usually worn by older persons.

Das ciptoning-*Muster zeigt
Figuren des Schattentheaters
(*wayang*) auf dem Muster
dele kecer („verstreute
Sojabohnen"). Wayang-Figu-
ren stehen für Weisheit und
Erfahrung, daher werden
Röcke mit solchen Mustern
oft von älteren Personen
getragen.*

10
Skirt *kain panjang*
Sultan's court (*kraton*)
at Yogyakarta
Central Java, 1930-1935
246 x 103 cm

The design *ciptoning* represents shadow theatre marionettes *(wayang)* placed on
the *dele kecer* design ("scat-
tered soy beans"). *Wayang*
figures indicate wisdom and
experience and therefore
skirts with such designs are
usually worn by older persons.

Das ciptoning-*Muster zeigt*
Figuren des Schattentheaters
(wayang) *auf dem Muster*
dele kecer *(„verstreute*
Sojabohnen"). Wayang-Figu-
ren stehen für Weisheit und
Erfahrung, daher werden
Röcke mit solchen Mustern
oft von älteren Personen
getragen.

11
Skirt *kain panjang*
Purworejo
Central Java, 1930-1935
cotton and gold leaf (*prada*)
240 x 95 cm

Batik skirts with designs of
marionettes from the shadow
theatre (*wayang*) are usually
worn by older persons. The
application of gold leaf
(*prada*) makes this fabric suitable for the celebration of
most important events, such
as weddings.

Batikröcke mit Figuren aus
dem Schattentheater
(wayang) *werden meist von*
älteren Leuten getragen.
Wegen des Goldauftrags
(prada) *eignet sich dieser*
Stoff für Feiern zu wichtigen
Anlässen, z. B. Hochzeiten.

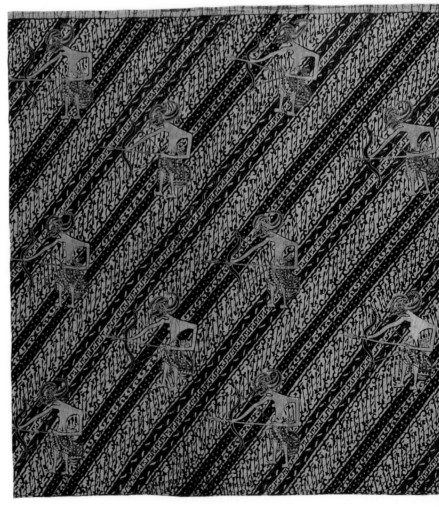

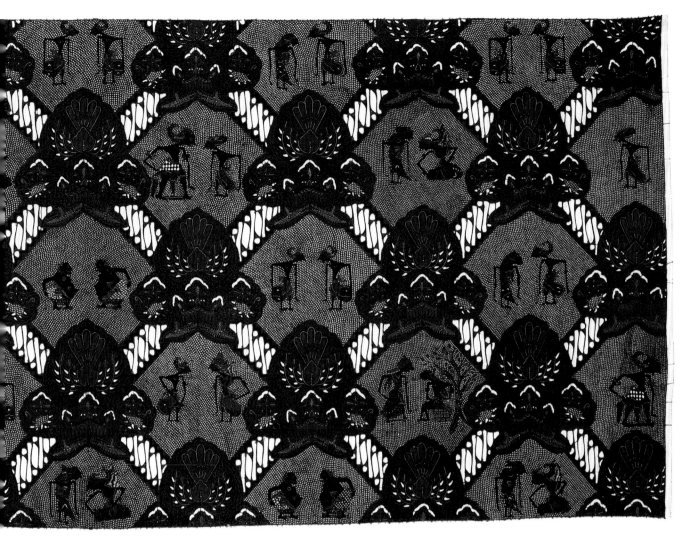

12
Head-cover *iket kepala*
Paku Alaman court
(second court), Yogyakarta
Central Java, 1925-1930
103 x 103 cm

Motif *lar* - single wing of the mythical bird *Garuda*, has been interspersed with the *sembagen huk* (small circle with a phoenix). Both designs are associated with persons of the highest social status.

Zwischen den lar - *Motiven - einzelne Flügel des mythologischen Vogels* Garuda - *wurde das* sembagen huk *(kleiner Kreis mit Phönix) eingefügt. Beide Muster stehen mit Personen des höchsten sozialen Ranges in Verbindung.*

13
Breast-cloth *kemben*
Sultan's court (*kraton*)
at Yogyakarta
Central Java, 1930-1935
52 x 260 cm

The cloth is worn tightly
wrapped around the torso.
The uniform decorative
design known as *byur* is suitable for unmarried women.

*Das Brusttuch wurde fest um
den Oberkörper gewickelt.
Das einheitliche, dekorative
Muster nennt sich* byur *und
wird von unverheirateten
Frauen getragen.*

14
Breast-cloth *kemben*
Sultan's court (*kraton*) at
Yogyakarta
Central Java, 1910-1915
cotton and silk appliqué
53 x 261 cm

Married women at the Cen-
tral-Javanese courts wear a
breast-cover with an elongated central field, covered with
fine silk. The elongated, diamond-like figure (*sidangan*)
indicates their wedded status.
(nos. 14 - 17)

An den zentraljavanischen
Höfen tragen verheiratete
Frauen ein Brusttuch mit
langgestrecktem zentralen
Feld, das mit Seide abgesetzt
ist. Die langgezogene, rauten-
ähnliche Form (sidangan)
weist auf den Status als Ehe-
frau hin. (Nr. 14 - 17)

15
Breast-cloth *kemben*
Sultan's court (*kraton*)
at Yogyakarta
Central Java, 1910-1915
cotton and silk appliqué
52 x 260 cm

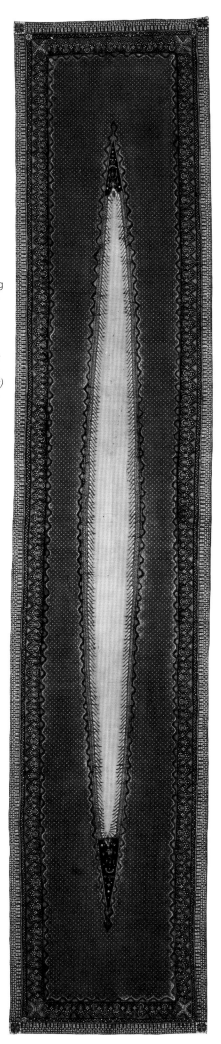

16
Breast-cloth *kemben*
Yogyakarta
Central Java, 1930-1935
cotton and silk appliqué
batik
plangi and *tritik* technique
50 x 255 cm

Breast-cloths decorated with
a combination of resist-dyeing
techniques: batik, *plangi* (tie-
dye) and *tritik* (stitch-dyeing)
are known as kain *kembangan* ("flowered cloths").

*Brusttücher mit Musterung in
mehreren Reservetechniken -
batik,* plangi *(Abbindetechnik)
und* tritik *(Nähreservierung) -
heißen kain kembangan
(„geblümter Stoff").*

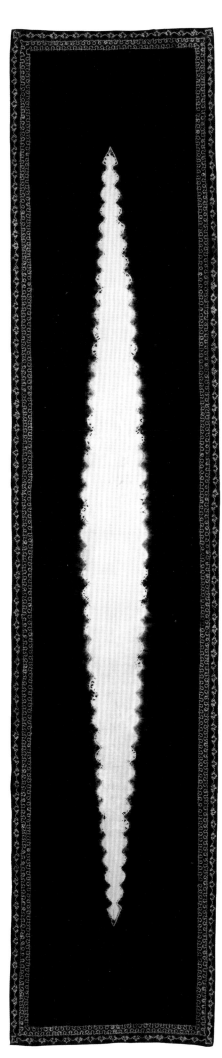

17
Breast-cloth *kemben*
Central Java, 1930-1935
tritik (stitch-dyeing) technique
52 x 249 cm

Black and white *kemben* are
known as *bangun tulak* and
worn as protective cloths.

Schwarz-weiße kemben *heißen* bangun tulak *und werden als schutzspendende
Tücher getragen.*

18
Ceremonial cloth
kain dodot
Yogyakarta
Central Java, 1930-1935
351 x 236 cm

The cloth has been decorated with the *semen* design - a stylised rendition of a sacred landscape, composed of mountains, trees, snakes, birds and small pavilions.

Dieses Tuch trägt das semen-Muster - die stilisierte Darstellung einer heiligen Landschaft mit Bergen, Bäumen, Schlangen, Vögeln und kleinen Pavillons.

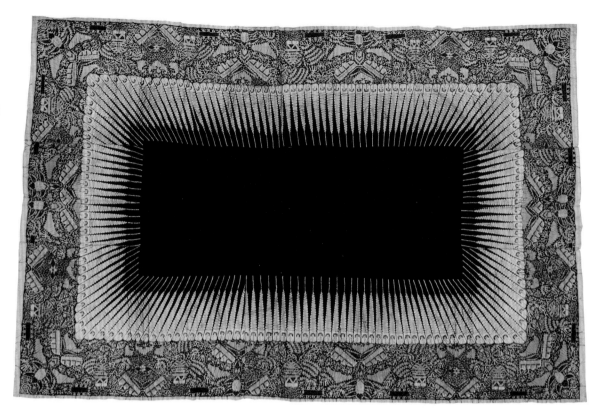

19
Ceremonial cloth
kain dodot
Yogyakarta
Central Java, 1930-1935
394 x 236 cm

A garment of this type is worn as a ceremonial skirt by the rulers of Yogyakarta and Surakarta, as well as by a bride and groom during their wedding; decorated with a design from the *parang* group.

Diese Art Kleidungsstück tragen die Herrscher in Yogyakarta und Surakarta als Zeremonialrock sowie Braut und Bräutigam bei der Hochzeit; Musterung mit einem Motiv aus der parang-Gruppe.

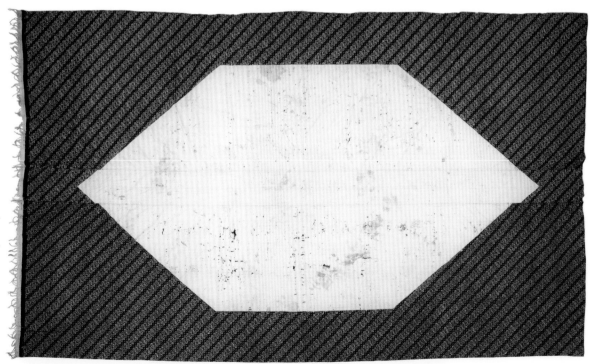

20
Skirt *sarong*
Surakarta,
Central Java, 1930-1935
203 x 106 cm

While the front of the skirt
features a dramatic composition, being a free interpretation of an old *tumpal* design
(row of triangles), the main
part has been decorated with
the *sido luhur* design (associated with a happy, noble life),
used as a background for
large, freely-drawn floral
bouquets.

*Die Vorderseite dieses Rockes
zeigt eine dramatische Komposition: eine freie Interpretation des alten* tumpal-*Musters
(Reihe von Dreiecken). Der
Hauptteil zeigt das* sido luhur-
*Muster, das man mit einem
glücklichen und erhabenen
Leben in Verbindung bringt.
Das Muster bildet den Hintergrund für große, frei gezeich-
nete Blumensträuße.*

21
Skirt *sarong*
Surakarta
Central Java, 1910-1920
222 x 105 cm

The composition of the front panel - *kepala* ("head") indicates European influence (baskets of flowers), while the main part of the cloth - *badan* ("body") has been decorated with *sawat* - one of the most prominent Central Javanese designs.

Die Komposition des vorderen Feldes, des kepala („Kopfes"), weist auf europäische Einflüsse hin (Körbe mit Blumen), der Hauptteil des Tuchs dagegen, der badan („Körper"), zeigt das sawat, eines der wichtigsten Muster Zentraljavas.

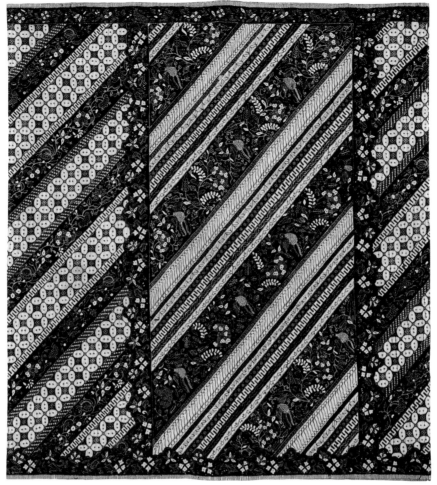

22
Skirt *sarong*
Yogyakarta
Central Java, 1930-1935
192 x 105 cm

On Central Java the *sarong* is worn as an informal, everyday dress. Its decoration features diagonal bands of the *kawung* design (four-petal flower design) interspersed with birds and floral motifs.

In Zentraljava trägt man den sarong *als zwanglose Alltagskleidung. Die Ornamentierung zeigt diagonale Streifen mit* kawung-*Muster (vierblättrige Blüte), dazwischen Vögel und florale Motive.*

23
Sash *selendang*
Lasem
North Java, 1900-1910
62 x 200 cm

The decoration of the cloth indicates the strong influence of the composition of Indian chintz textiles, especially the tree of life design with opened, variegated blossoms.

Die Ornamentierung des Tuches zeigt deutliche Einflüsse aus der Komposition indischer Chintze, hier insbesondere das Motiv des Lebensbaumes mit offenen, panaschierten Blüten.

24
Skirt *sarong*
Lasem
North Java, 1900 - 1910
198 x 106 cm

The design of this exquisite *kain laseman* indicates the influence of Indian chintz textiles as well as Chinese iconography. Skirts of this kind used to be worn by Chinese and Indo-European women from the north coast of Java.

Das Muster dieses exquisiten kain laseman *weist auf Einflüsse indischer Chintze und der chinesischen Ikonografie hin. Derartige Röcke wurden von Chinesinnen und indo-europäischen Frauen an der Nordküste Javas getragen.*

25
Skirt *sarong*
Lasem
North Java, 1900 - 1910
198 x 105 cm

The *kepala* - "head" features two parrots, while the *badan* - "body" (main part of the skirt), is decorated with the tree of life design with oversized flowers and fantastic birds. The large, variously patterned petals were a characteristic feature of Indian chintz textiles produced for European market.

Der kepala - „Kopf" - zeigt zwei Papageien, der badan - „Körper" (Hauptteil des Rocks) - trägt das Motiv des Lebensbaumes mit übergroßen Blumen und Fantasievögeln. Die großen, verschiedenartig gemusterten Blütenblätter waren ein typisches Merkmal indischer Chintzstoffe für den europäischen Markt.

26
Skirt *sarong*
Lasem
North Java, 1900-1910
208 x 107 cm

27
Skirt *sarong*
Lasem
North Java, 1900-1910
198 x 105 cm

28
Skirt *kain panjang*
Lasem or Semarang
North Java, 1920-1925
181 x 102 cm

The skirt is decorated with a range of animals which are not native to Java, such as elephants, camels and lions.

Der Rock trägt eine Reihe von in Java nicht heimischen Tieren, z.B. Elefanten, Kamele und Löwen.

29
Skirt *sarong*
Lasem
North Java, 1900-1910
196 x 106 cm

30
Skirt *sarong*
Lasem
North Java, 1900 - 1910
215 x 106 cm

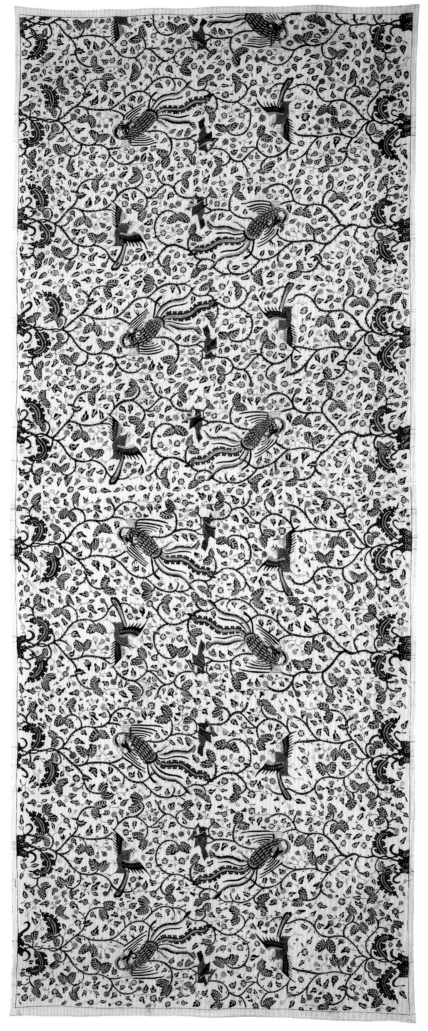

35
Skirt *kain panjang*
Lasem or Semarang
North Java, 1930-1935
261 x 106 cm

Cloth without red colour,
representing in dark blue the
typical *laseman* design - blossoming trees, surrounded by
birds of paradise and phoenixes, was known as *kain
kelengan*. This type of garment was used as a mour-
ning dress by the Chinese
population of North Java.

*Tücher ohne rote Farbe, die
das typische* laseman-*Muster
- blühende Bäume umgeben
von Paradiesvögeln und
Phönixen - in Dunkelblau
zeigten, hießen* kain kelengan. *Solche Kleidungsstücke
wurden von der chinesischen
Bevölkerung Nordjavas als
Trauerkleidung getragen.*

36
Skirt *kain panjang*
Javanese Chinese workshop
Lasem or Semarang
North Java, 1910-1920
252 x 104 cm

This carefully executed kain
has been decorated with a
range of auspicious creatures
and a frequently repeated
motif of pomegranate fruit,
the numerous seeds of which
are recognised as a symbol of
fertility.

*Die Musterung dieses sorg-
fältig ausgeführten kain zeigt
verschiedene Glück bringende
Wesen sowie das häufig wie-
derholte Motiv des Granat-
apfels, dessen zahlreiche
Samen als Fruchtbarkeits-
symbol gelten.*

37
Skirt *sarong*
Lasem
North Java, 1890 - 1900
211 x 106 cm

The main field of the skirt features a stylised inscription: "SLAMET NJANG PAKE" - "Luck / blessing for the owner / wearer"

Das Hauptfeld dieses Rocks zeigt eine stilisierte Inschrift: „SLAMET NJANG PAKE" - „Glück / Segen der Trägerin / dem Besitzer".

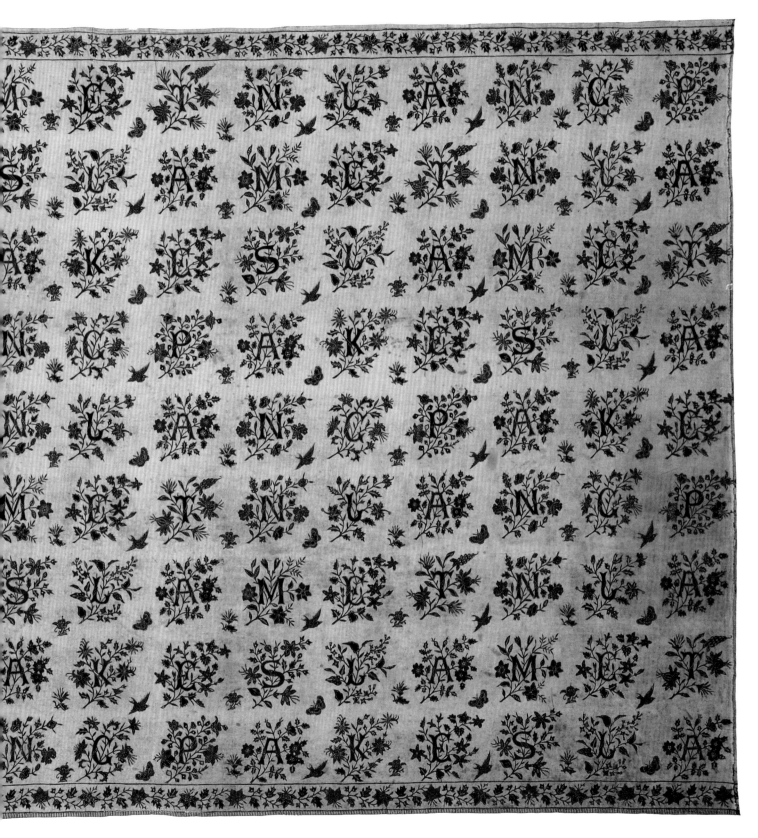

38
Skirt *sarong*
Lasem
North Java, 1895-1900
181 x 106 cm

This batik reveals a fascina-
tion with the latest means of
travel - be it bicycle, automo-
bile or aeroplane, rendered in
wax in the impeccable *laseman* style.

*Diese Batik zeigt die Faszina-
tion für die neuesten Verkehrsmittel, wie Fahrrad, Automobil
oder Flugzeug. Alle wurden
mit Wachs im fehlerlosen lase-
man-Stil ausgeführt.*

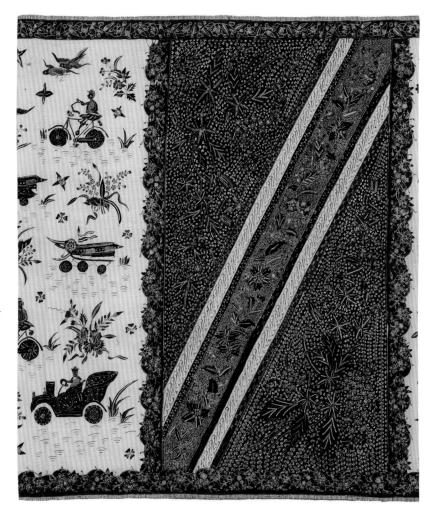

39
Skirt *sarong*
Cirebon or Semarang
North Java, 1860-1870
205 x 105 cm

This exquisite batiked skirt was decorated with a very fine version of *tambal* - the patchwork design, deemed to have protective powers. The cloth has been further enhanced by being covered with a layer of gold leaf - *prada*. (See preface).

Dieser exquisite Batikrock zeigt eine sehr schöne Version des tambal, *des Patchwork-Musters, dem man schützende Kräfte zuschrieb. Das Tuch wurde durch einen Goldauftrag -* prada - *weiter verschönert. (Siehe Vorwort).*

40
Trousers *celana*
Pekalongan
North Java, 1925-1930
125 x 106 cm

41
Trousers *celana*
Lasem
North Java, 1920-1930
120 x 104 cm

Unlike the Javanese, the Chinese and European residents at home used to wear not a *sarong* but batiked trousers. This pair, probably for a Chinese man, has been decorated with two powerful dragon designs.

Im Gegensatz zu den Javanern trugen chinesische und europäische Einwohner Zuhause nicht unbedingt einen sarong, *sondern oft auch Batikhosen. Diese Hose, vermutlich für einen chinesischen Mann gefertigt, zieren zwei mächtige Drachenmotive.*

42
Skirt *sarong*
North Java, 1920-1930
126 x 103 cm (fragment)

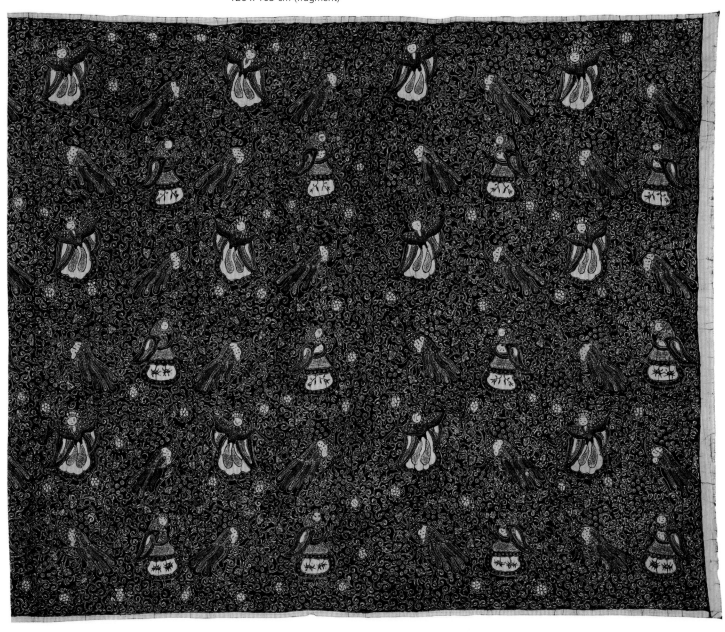

Fragment of a skirt, probably a sarong, featuring joyful, floating angels interspaced with birds. Probably it was worn by a woman of mixed, Javanese-European background.

Rockfragment, vermutlich eines Sarongs, mit fröhlichen, schwebenden Engeln und alternierend Vögeln. Wahrscheinlich trug ihn eine Frau javanisch-europäischer Abstammung.

43
Skirt *sarong*
Pekalongan
North Java, 1900 - 1910
signed:
"Mrs.G.T.JAN.PEKALONGAN"
199 x 105 cm

The *kepala* section features two peacocks among blossoming branches, while the *badan* - the main part of the skirt - has been decorated with human beings with wings.

Der kepala-*Teil zeigt zwei Pfauen zwischen blühenden Zweigen, den* badan - *den Hauptteil des Rockes - zieren menschliche Gestalten mit Flügeln.*

44
Skirt *sarong*
Pekalongan
North Java, 1910-1915
workshop of Lien Metzelaar
(c.1855-1930),
signed: "L. Metz Pek"
219 x 108 cm

Fairy-tales were one of the
favourite topics appearing on
batiked skirts worn by young
women of the Javanese-
European group. The story of
Cinderella appears on skirts
produced in a number of
Pekalongan workshops.

*Märchen waren für die Batik-
röcke junger Frauen der java-
nisch-europäischen Bevöl-
kerungsgruppe ein Lieblings-
thema. Die Geschichte von
Aschenputtel erscheint auf
Röcken aus verschiedenen
Werkstätten Pekalongans.*

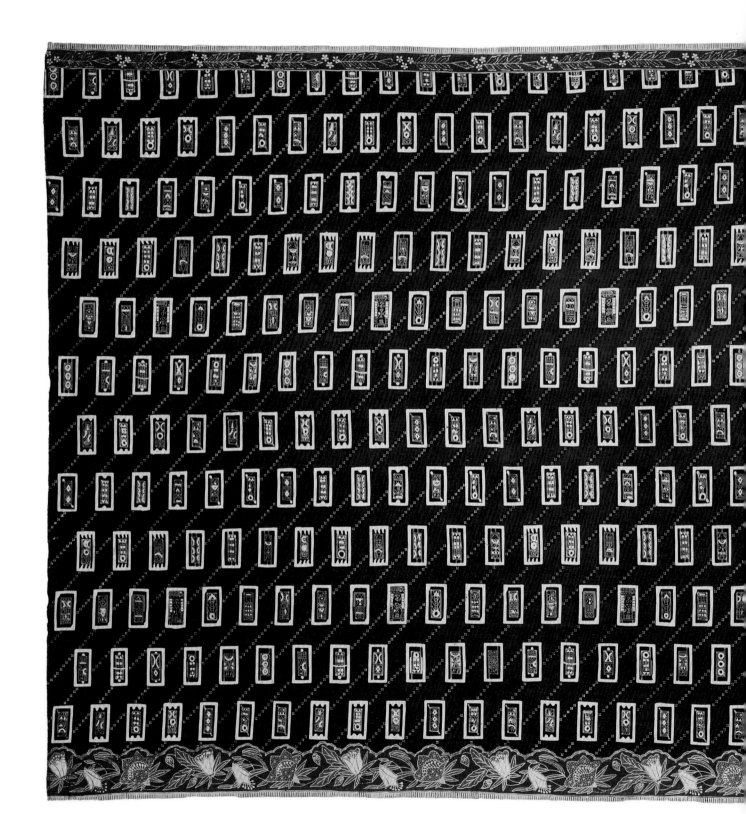

45
Skirt *sarong*
Pekalongan
North Java, 1910-1915
workshop of Lien Metzelaar
(c. 1855-1930)
signed: "L. Metz Pek"
214 x 108 cm

The main part of the fabric features *cherki* cards - perhaps a favourite game of the owner of the skirt?

Der Hauptteil des Stoffes zeigt Cherki-*Karten, vielleicht das Lieblingsspiel der Rock-besitzerin?*

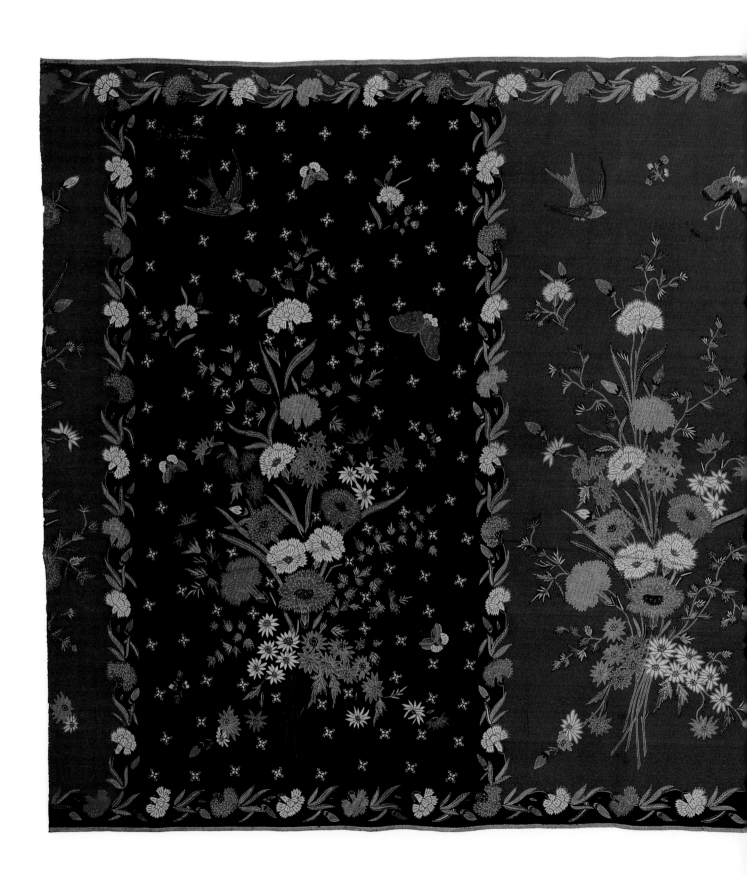

46
Skirt *sarong*
Pekalongan
North Java, 1930-1935
workshop of Eliza van Zuylen
(1863-1947)
signed: "E v Zuylen"
206 x 107 cm

Bouquets of flowers, executed with great care for detail,
were the trademark of the
Eliza van Zuylen workshop -
probably the longest running
Indo-European workshop at
Pekalongan.

*Mit großer Detailgenauigkeit
ausgeführte Blumensträuße
waren das Markenzeichen der
Werkstatt Eliza van Zuylen, der
wahrscheinlich am längsten
bestehenden indo-europäischen
Werkstatt von Pekalongan.*

47
Skirt *sarong*
Pekalongan
North Java, 1910-1915
workshop of Eliza van Zuylen
(1863-1947)
signed: "E v Zuylen"
217 x 105 cm

A "novel" approach towards
the composition of this
sarong is indicated by a large
diagonal band decorating the
kepala section, with symmetrical arrangements of carnations. The main field, *badan*,
features groups of irises.

*Der große diagonale Streifen
im kepala-Bereich und die
symetrisch angeordneten
Nelken weisen auf eine „neuartige" Vorgehensweise bei
der Komposition dieses
sarongs hin. Das Hauptfeld
badan zeigt Gruppen von Iris.*

48
Skirt *sarong*
Pekalongan
North Java, 1910 - 1915
workshop of Eliza van Zuylen
(1863 - 1947)
signed: "E v Zuylen"
210 x 106 cm

Another version of the bouquet of flowers from the van Zuylen workshop. Special care was given to the execution of the background design covering the field of *badan*.

Eine weitere Version des Blumenstraußes aus der Werkstatt van Zuylen. Das Hintergrundmuster im Feld des badan *ist mit besonderer Sorgfalt ausgeführt.*

49
Skirt *sarong*
Pekalongan
North Java, 1910-1915
workshop of A.J.F. Jans
(c. 1850 - c. 1920)
signed: "J.Jans"
216 x 107 cm

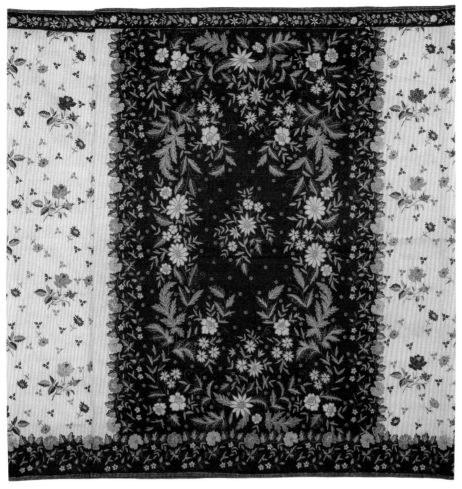

50
Skirt *sarong*
Pekalongan
North Java, 1885-1900
workshop of A.J.F. Jans
(c. 1850 - c. 1920)
signed: "Wed.J.Jans No.2"
209 x 106 cm

Mrs Jans was the only owner
of a major batik workshop in
Pekalongan whose parents
were both Dutch. Following
the death of her husband in
1885, for a number of years
she used to sign her batiks
as Wed.J.Jans - *weduve*
("widow") J.Jans.

Frau Jans war die einzige Be-
sitzerin einer größeren Batik-
werkstatt in Pekalongan,
deren Eltern beide Holländer
waren. Nach dem Tod ihres
Ehemannes 1885 signierte sie
einige Jahre lang ihre Batiken
mit Wed.J.Jans - weduve
("Witwe") J.Jans.

51
Skirt *sarong*
Pekalongan
North Java, 1910-1915
workshop of A.J.F. Jans
(c. 1850 - c. 1920)
signed: "J.Jans"
215 x 106 cm

52
Skirt *sarong*
Pekalongan
North Java, 1900-1910
workshop of A.J.F. Jans
(c. 1850 - c. 1920)
signed: "J.Jans"
198 x 106 cm

53
Skirt *sarong*
Pekalongan
North Java, 1880-1885
workshop of B. Fisßer
(c. 1825-1905)
signed: "Mevr.B.Fisßer
Pekalongan"
204 x 107 cm

Mrs B. Fisßer was probably
the first Indo-European producer of batiks in Pekalongan
to start signing her fabrics.

*Frau B. Fisßer war vermutlich
die erste indo-europäische
Batikherstellerin in Pekalongan, die mit dem Signieren
ihrer Stoffe begann.*

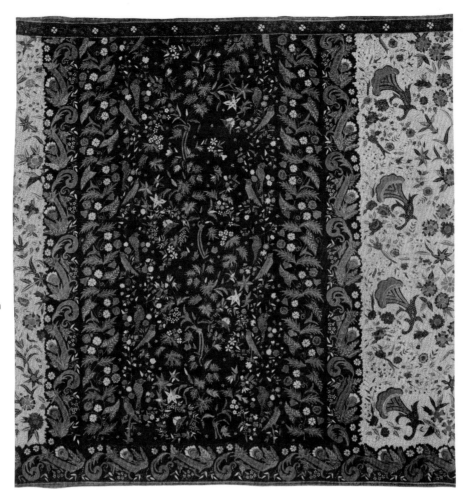

54
Skirt *sarong*
Pekalongan or Semarang
North Java, 1900-1910
214 x 108 cm

Another rendition of the
popular floral topic from
Pekalongan: this time the
badan features baskets of
flowers, while the decorative
border is composed of pot-
plants.

*Eine weitere Umsetzung des
beliebten floralen Themas von
Pekalongan: Diesmal zeigt der
badan Körbe mit Blumen,
während die dekorative
Bordüre aus Topfpflanzen
besteht.*

55
Skirt *sarong*
North Java, 1890 - 1895
212 x 122 cm

The ornate, free-flowing floral design of the *badan* indicates the influence of European textiles of 18th century, especially the rocaille design.
The owner of this *sarong was a tall person, hence a strip of fabric 18 cm in width has been added to the upper edge.*

Das kunstvolle, frei fließende florale Muster des badan, *und insbesondere das Rocaille-Muster, zeigen den Einfluss europäischer Textilien des 18. Jahrhunderts.
Der Besitzer des* sarong *war eine große Person, daher der angesetzte Stoffstreifen von 18 cm an der oberen Kante.*

56
Skirt *sarong*
Sidoharjo
East Java, 1910-1920
195 x 105 cm

Large bouquets of flowers -
this typical Pekalongan design
was probably produced by a
batik workshop situated in
another town of East Java.

*Große Blumensträuße - dieses
typische Muster von Pekalongan wurde vermutlich in einer
Batikwerkstatt einer anderen
Stadt Ostjavas gefertigt.*

57
Skirt *sarong*
Pekalongan
North Java, c. 1920
workshop of The Tie Siet
signed: "The Tie Siet,
Pekalongan"
204 x 104 cm

Chinese interpretation of the
famous floral theme of Pekalongan. While peonies feature
in the field of *kepala*, the
badan has been decorated
with rows of carnations.

*Chinesische Interpretation des
berühmten floralen Themas
von Pekalongan. Im Feld des
kepala sind Päonien (Pfingstrosen) zu sehen, den badan
schmücken Reihen von
Nelken.*

58
Skirt *sarong*
Pekalongan
North Java, c. 1920
workshop of The Tie Siet
signed: "The Tie Siet,
Pekalongan"
200 x 106 cm

At the beginning of the 20th
century, encouraged by the
success of the "bouquet"
sarongs from Indo-European
workshops, Chinese work-
shops at Pekalongan also
introduced this design to their
repertoire. In many cases,
Chinese clients opted for a
lighter, pastel range of
colours.

Ermutigt durch den Erfolg der
sarongs *mit Blumensträußen*
aus den indo-europäischen
Werkstätten, nahmen chinesi-
sche Werkstätten Anfang des
20. Jahrhunderts dieses Motiv
ebenfalls in ihr Repertoire auf.
Oft wählten die chinesischen
Kunden eine hellere Farbge-
bung mit Pastelltönen.

59
Table-cloth
Pekalongan
North Java, 1930-1935
102 x 102 cm

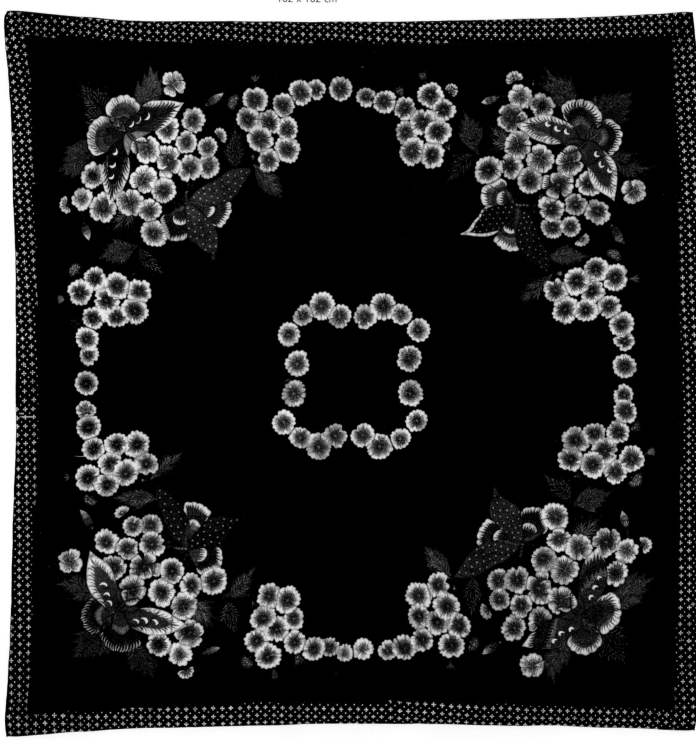

Besides garments, some of the Indo-European batik workshops used to produce a range of decorative fabrics, such as serviettes, table-cloths, wall-hangings, etc.

Neben Kleidungsstücken produzierten manche indo-europäische Batikwerkstätten eine Reihe von Dekorationsstoffen wie Servietten, Tischdecken, Wandbehänge etc.

60
Skirt *sarong*
Kudus
North Java, 1930-1935
workshop of
Nyonya (Mrs) Lie Boen In
signed: "Koedoes,
Nja Lie Boen In"
213 x 107 cm

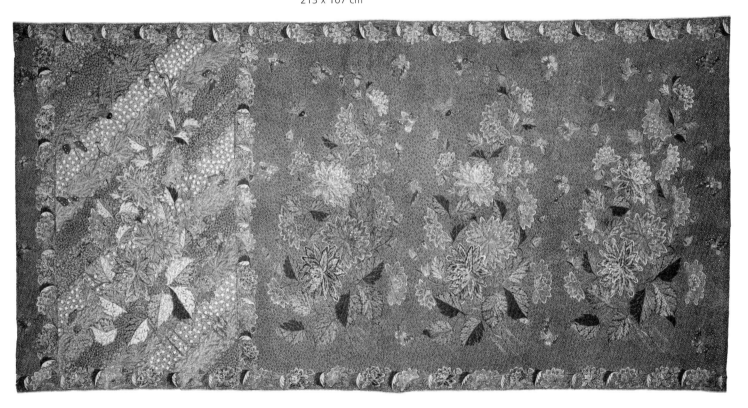

Chinese workshops at Kudus specialised in the rendering of the famous Pekalongan design of bouquets of flowers placed on a densely filled background. Peonies and chrysanthemums, favoured by Chinese clients, replaced European flowers.

Chinesische Werkstätten in Kudus spezialisierten sich auf eine Ausführung des berühmten Blumenstrauß-Musters von Pekalongan auf dicht gefülltem Hintergrund. Chinesische Kunden bevorzugten Päonien und Chrysanthemen anstelle europäischer Blumen.

61
Skirt *kain*
Kudus
North Java, 1930-1935
workshop of
Nyonya (Mrs) Lie Boen In
signed: "Koedoes,
Nja Lie Boen In"
257 x 108 cm

The composition of this skirt features the *pagi sore* ("morning and afternoon") arrangement. The cloth has been divided diagonally, featuring two different halves, each of which could be displayed according to the preference of the wearer.

Die Komposition dieses Rockes zeigt das Arrangement pagi sore *("Vormittag und Nachmittag"). Das Tuch ist diagonal in zwei verschiedene Hälften geteilt, von denen je nach Tageszeit und Wunsch der Trägerin die eine oder die andere gezeigt werden konnte.*

62
Skirt *kain*
Kudus
North Java, 1930-1935
workshop of
Nyonya (Mrs) Lie Boen In
signed: "Koedoes,
Nja Lie Boen In"
265 x 107 cm

Another example of the *pagi sore* composition from Kudus, featuring a brown, densely filled background - the trade mark of batik workshops active in that area.

Ein weiteres Beispiel der pagi sore-*Komposition aus Kudus mit braunem, dicht gefülltem Hintergrund - das Markenzeichen der dort aktiven Batikwerkstätten.*

Used by Chinese women on Java to carry a ring of keys or small personal possessions, such as cloves or tobacco containers. It could be slung over the shoulder or tucked into the waistband.

Chinesinnen auf Java trugen in solchen Tüchern Schlüsselbunde oder kleine persönliche Gegenstände wie Gewürznelken- oder Tabaksbehälter. Sie konnten über die Schulter geschlungen oder in den Rockbund gesteckt werden.

Painting of a Peranakan lady from Cirebon, oil on canvas, c. 1880

64
Ceremonial hanging
Javanese Chinese workshop
Lasem or Semarang
North Java, 1910-1915
216 x 72 cm

The composition depicts
scenes from Chinese legends,
interspersed with the "tree of
life" design borrowed from
Indian trade cloths. Used as a
ceremonial cloth in a Chinese
house or a temple on Java.

*Die Komposition zeigt Szenen
aus chinesischen Legenden,
dazwischen das von indischen
Handelsstoffen entlehnte
Motiv des „Lebensbaumes".
Zeremonialtuch für ein chine-
sisches Haus oder einen
Tempel auf Java.*

65
Altar cloth *tok wi*
Javanese Chinese workshop
Lasem or Semarang
North Java, 1910 - 1920
104 x 104 cm

Almost every Chinese home on Java had an altar - the place for commemorating deities and ancestors. In China, altars used to be decorated with embroidered fabrics; on Java their place was taken by batik textiles, depicting scenes from legends, deities and auspicious symbols.

Fast jeder chinesische Haushalt auf Java hatte einen Altar als Gedenkort für die Götter und Ahnen. In China wurden Altäre mit bestickten Stoffen geschmückt, auf Java waren es Batiktextilien mit Szenen aus Legenden, Götterdarstellungen und Glückssymbolen.

66
Decorative hanging *mui li*
Javanese Chinese workshop
Lasem or Semarang
North Java, 1890 - 1910
215 x 104 cm

At the entrance to some
Chinese houses a protective
fabric with auspicious symbols was hung to ward off
evil forces and bring good
luck to the home.

*Bei manchen chinesischen
Häusern wurde ein Schutz
spendendes Tuch mit Glückssymbolen an den Eingang
gehängt, um böse Mächte
abzuwehren und dem Heim
Glück zu bringen.*

67
Bed cover *kain sprei*
Javanese Chinese workshop
Lasem or Semarang
North Java, 1910-1915
104 x 186 cm (Batik)
153 x 235 cm (total)

68
Bed cover *kain sprei*
Javanese Chinese workshop
Lasem or Semarang
North Java, 1900 - 1910
253 x 209 cm

69
Decorative hanging
Javanese Chinese workshop
Semarang
North Java, 1900-1910
Letters in the center:
"SAMARANG [...] T. JOWAH
[...]"
198 x 107 cm

72
Head-scarf *kudhung*
Cirebon
North Java or Sumatra
1910-1920
94 x 233 cm

(See no. 71)

73
Skirt *kain panjang*
North Java for export to
Sumatra or Jambi
Sumatra, early 20th century
257 x 108 cm

The market on Sumatra
favoured skirts featuring two
ends with a *tumpal* design
executed in different colours.
The main field, composed of
metrically repeated medalli-
ons, indicates the close similarity to *sembagi* textiles which
in the past used to be imported from India to Sumatra in
large quantities.

*Auf dem Markt von Sumatra
wurden Röcke mit verschie-
denfarbig ausgeführten tumpal-Mustern an den beiden
Enden bevorzugt. Das Hauptfeld mit den regelmäßig wiederholten Medaillons zeigt
eine enge Verwandtschaft mit
sembagi-Textilien, die früher
in großen Mengen von Indien
nach Sumatra eingeführt
wurden.*

74
Head-scarf *kudhung*
North Java for export to
Sumatra or Jambi
Sumatra, early 20th century
91 x 210 cm

Head-scarfs worn on Sumatra
were usually of a much larger
size than those on Java.
Sometimes their size almost
equalled these of batiked
skirts (see no. 75), however,
the fact that these fabrics lack
rows of *tumpal* designs, indicates that they were worn by
Muslim women as a head
and shoulder cover.

Die auf Sumatra getragenen
Kopftücher waren meist viel
größer als die javanischen.
Manchmal waren sie beinahe
so groß wie Batikröcke (siehe
Nr. 75), doch das Fehlen von
tumpal-Mustern auf diesen
Stoffen weist auf ihre
Verwendung als Kopf- und
Schultertuch für muslimische
Frauen hin.

75
Head-scarf *kudhung*
Chinese workshop at Lasem
for export to Sumatra
North Java, 1900-1910
90 x 217 cm

This type of cloth is known as
kain jupri, named after the
Arab Al Juffri family, a famous
entrepreneur from Jambi.
Made in Chinese-owned
workshops in Lasem for
Muslim women on Sumatra,
the motifs of the central field
clearly indicate the Chinese
origins of these fabrics.

Diese Art des Stoffes heißt
kain jupri, *benannt nach der
arabischen Familie Al Juffri,
einem berühmten Unter-
nehmer aus Jambi. Sie wurde
in chinesisch geführten Werkstätten in Lasem für muslimische Frauen auf Sumatra
gefertigt. Die Motive im zentralen Feld zeigen eindeutig
den chinesischen Ursprung
dieser Stoffe.*

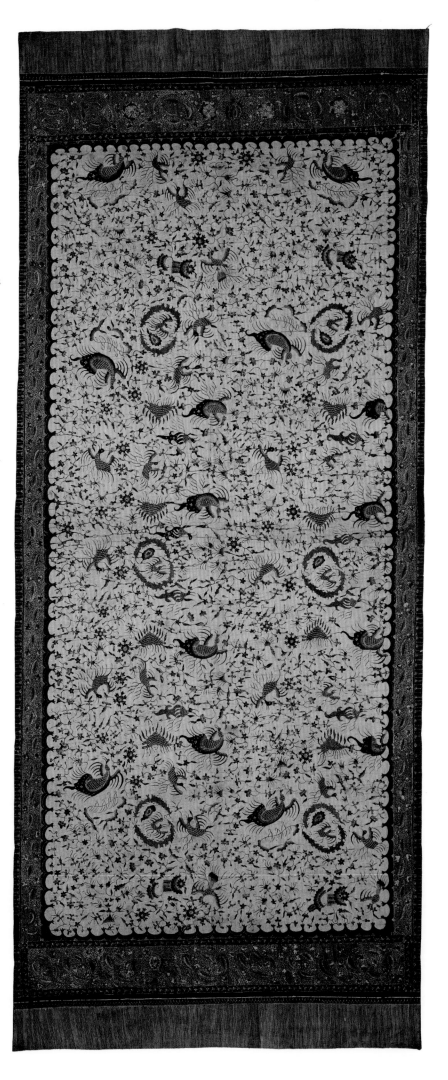

Portrait of a Peranakan lady
from Sumatra, oil on canvas,
c. 1880

Interview mit Rudolf G. Smend und Donald J. Harper

Donald Harper und Rudolf G. Smend
im Batikworkshop in Yogyakarta, 1985

Intern. Art Fair Cologne
6.-10. Nov. 1975

Herr Smend, Ihr erster Aufenthalt in Indonesien, dem Ursprungsland der Batiken, war ja eigentlich gar nicht geplant... Wie kam es, dass Sie damals dort hingelangten...

Eigentlich wollte ich 1972 mit meiner damaligen Lebensgefährtin nach Australien auswandern. Wir hatten die gesamte Strecke mit dem Auto bewältigt, viele Länder durchquert – da änderten sich kurzfristig die Einreisebedingungen für Australien. Je näher wir unserem eigentlichen Ziel kamen, desto mehr verlor es seinen Reiz – wir hörten ja auch nicht besonders viel Positives über dieses Land von den Auswanderern, denen wir begegneten. Dagegen schwärmten die Leute von Indonesien. Selbst dort angekommen, bestätigten sich die Informationen: Die Leute waren so freundlich, aufgeschlossen und spontan, das Leben war preiswert, das Klima angenehm. In Yogyakarta herrschte eine euphorische Aufbruchstimmung nach der Soekarno-Ära, wirtschaftlich gab es kleine Fortschritte, der Tourismus begann gerade wieder. Wir änderten also spontan unser Ziel und blieben in Indonesien.

Wann kamen Sie zum ersten Mal bewusst mit Batiken in Kontakt?

Das war in Yogyakarta, auf Java. Wir hatten inzwischen davon gehört, dass diese Stadt das Batik-Zentrum Indonesiens sei. Kulturellem gegenüber stets aufgeschlossen und neugierig suchten wir das so genannte Wasserschloss des Sultans auf, in dem es einige anscheinend gerade neu eröffnete „Batik-Galerien" gab. Dort wurden die neu entdeckten „batik-paintings" ausgestellt – Bilder z. B. in surrealistischem Stil, ausgeführt aber in der traditionellen Batiktechnik. Mit einem dieser Batikkünstler – Gianto – freundeten wir uns an und er brachte uns über eine Woche lang den Umgang mit dem Canting, mit Wachs und den lichtechten und kochfesten Farben in Pulverform bei. Diese kamen zu unserer großen Überraschung aus Deutschland... Da waren wir bald eine geschäftsfördernde Attraktion für unseren Freund: zwei Deutsche auf kleinen Höckerchen sitzend, bei den ersten Versuchen, die Batikkunst zu erlernen – ja... Nachdem wir Einblick in die Technik hatten, konnten wir die Kunstfertigkeit und den Wert der einheimischen Ergebnisse erst so richtig schätzen und die Preise dafür erschienen uns unglaublich günstig. Da Gianto für seinen Unterricht kein Geld annehmen wollte, kauften wir zum Abschied einige seiner Bilder.

Da waren sie aber von der Sammelleidenschaft historischer Batiken noch weit entfernt...

Ja, sicher. Das bewusste Sammeln alter Batiktextilien begann erst viel später – über den Umweg unserer Idee, eine Batik-Galerie in Deutschland zu eröffnen. Auf diese Idee wiederum kamen wir während der weiteren Reise bei unserem Aufenthalt auf Bali. Dort hatten wir unsere karge Unterkunft mit den Batikbildern von Gianto geschmückt – es sah schon beinahe aus wie eine Batik-Galerie. Wir registrierten die große Resonanz bei unseren europäischen Zimmernachbarn, machten Werbung für Gianto und seine Kunst, erklärten die Technik, soweit wir sie erlernt hatten. Ja, ich glaube, hier kam uns zum ersten Mal der Gedanke, in Köln selbst eine Art Batik-Galerie zu eröffnen: einen Teeladen, wie sie damals „in" waren, in dem man etwas von der Gastfreundschaft weitergeben konnte, die man auf der Reise erfahren hatte, in dem man sich wohl fühlen konnte... Nach Australien auszuwandern hatte seinen Reiz verloren, das Visum für Indonesien lief bald ab – und wir hatten tatsächlich etwas Heimweh... Zurück auf Java stellten wir eine Kollektion von 50 Batik-Bildern zusammen. Da das Budget begrenzt war, mussten wir sehr sorgfältig auswählen und uns informieren: Wir besuchten alle wichtigen Batik-Manufakturen, lernten im staatlichen Batik-Research-Institut Details über die Batik-Tradition. Am Ende kehrten wir nach Deutschland zurück mit einem guten Fundus an modernen und traditionellen Batiken verschiedener Größen und mit unterschiedlichsten Motiven.

Ganz offensichtlich war die Batik-Galerie ein Erfolg, denn sie bildete ja die Ausgangsbasis für Ihre heutige Textilgalerie...

Ja, wenn man bedenkt – eine großartige Geschäftsidee steckte bei der Gründung unserer Batik-Galerie 1973 nicht dahinter. Aber es lief zu unserer eigenen Überraschung richtig gut. Zur Eröffnung kamen vor allem Freunde und Bekannte – man hatte ja auch viel zu erzählen... Vorher hatten wir in allen Cafés und Kneipen in der Südstadt Werbung gemacht. Im Nachhinein muss man sagen, dass die Idee zur „Batik-Galerie" genau zum richtigen Zeitpunkt kam. Damals gab es eine Sehnsucht, eine Hoffnung für alles, was „aus dem Osten" kam. Dabei dachte man insbesondere an Indien als eine Art Heilsbringer. Wir kennen die Fotos der Beatles bei ihrem Guru, das legendäre „Concert for Bangladesh"; wir erinnern uns an die Sanyassins, die im Ashram in Poona wohnten und sich möglichst oft mit ihrem Meister Baghwan trafen.

Hier in Köln hatte der inzwischen legendäre Harry Owens 1972 einen Flohmarkt ins Leben gerufen, und die Idee wurde rasch in Düsseldorf, Bonn und Aachen aufgegriffen. Für ein „start up-Unternehmen" wie die völlig unbekannte Batik-Galerie waren diese Flohmärkte das ideale Medium. Dorthin kamen alle Schichten der Bevölkerung und man konnte nicht nur seine Produkte sondern auch sich selber testen. Allerdings ging es mir damals ganz einfach darum, mit meinem einzigen Kapital – den im Rucksack mitgebrachten 50 Batik-Bildern, von deren Qualität ich fest überzeugt war – Geld zu verdienen.

Wie wurden Batiktextilien damals in Deutschland eingestuft – wie war die Resonanz hier auf Ihre Vorliebe, Ihre „Geschäftsidee"?

Die Resonanz war sozusagen geteilt. Ich selbst war so überzeugt von der Kunst der Batik, dass ich mich um eine Teilnahme am Internationalen Kunst Markt – IKM – bewarb, den Ingo Kümmel 1973 in Düsseldorf ins Leben gerufen hatte: eine Protestveranstaltung gegen die Kölner Kunstmesse, zu der er mit seinem Galerie-Programm nicht zugelassen worden war. Er konnte viele erstklassige Galerien für sein Projekt begeistern. Ich befand mich letztlich mit meinem Stand neben der Galerie Krugier aus der Schweiz, die mit erstklassiger Kunst handelt. Krugier fand die Nachbarschaft zu indonesischen Hahnenkampf- und Ramayana Motiven auf Batik weniger passend: Sie sammelte Unterschriften gegen eine Teilnahme der Batik-Galerie an den zukünftigen Messen. Das brachte unserem Stand jedenfalls viel Aufmerksamkeit, das NRW-Fernsehen zeigte unsere recht farbenfrohen Batiken. Zum Glück brachte der Wirbel auch einige Käufer, so dass für mich die Messe insgesamt doch ein Erfolg war. 1974 habe ich auf derselben Messe übrigens wieder ausgestellt, allerdings nicht neben Krugier...

Auf derselben Kunstmesse hatte mich eine Besucherin entdeckt, die selbst Batiken herstellte. Bis dahin wusste ich gar nicht, dass diese „Kunstrichtung" in Deutschland gelehrt wurde und dass es eine „Batikwelle" zu Kaisers Zeiten und noch einmal nach dem Zweiten Weltkrieg gegeben hatte. Der Mann dieser Besucherin und Batik-Expertin war zu der Zeit Vorstandsmitglied der Dresdner Bank in Köln. Vielleicht aus einem

„Helfer-Syndrom" heraus, vielleicht aufgrund ihrer Liebe zur Batik: Jedenfalls vermittelte sie diesem Galeristen mit dem etwas anderen Programm den Kontakt zur PR-Abteilung der Dresdner Bank in Köln. Dort begeisterte man sich für die exotischen Batiken, die offensichtlich genau das Richtige waren, um in den Kassenhallen der Bank-Filialen ausgestellt zu werden. Ich lernte bei der Gelegenheit, wie man Eröffnungen inszeniert, wie man Presse-Arbeit macht, wie Einladungen und Infoblätter aussehen müssen und achtete natürlich besonders darauf, dass die Adresse der Batik-Galerie überall gut zu sehen war.

Im Großen und Ganzen fühlte ich mich durch diese Ereignisse in meiner Idee der Batik-Galerie bestärkt und reiste letztlich wieder nach Java, um die Künstler zu besuchen und passende Batik-Bilder für mein Galerie-Programm zu kaufen.

Gab es denn ein Schlüsselerlebnis, das Sie als den Beginn ihres Interesses an historischen Batiken und des Sammelns derselben bezeichnen würden?

Ja, ich wurde erstmals ganz bewusst auf historische Batiken aufmerksam über den Kontakt zu Ardiyanto, einem Chinesen, bei dem ich seit 1973 gerne Batiken einkaufte.

Bei einem meiner Besuche – das war 1976 – war ich zufällig Zeuge, als ihm ein Händler alte Batiken zeigte, die Ardiyanto mit Kennerblick durchsah, letztlich jedoch nichts davon kaufte. Die Unterhaltung ging natürlich auf indonesisch. Ich verstand nicht sehr viel, erkannte aber rasch, dass diese Batiken besonders schön waren. So etwas hatte ich noch nie gesehen – ich wusste gar nicht, dass es derartige Textilien überhaupt gab. Auf der Straße und auf den Märkten sah man ja lediglich die gewöhnlichen Batiken, nicht jene der „upper class". Die wunderbaren Stoffe des Händlers beeindruckten mich dermaßen, dass ich ihn nach Namen und Adresse fragte. Die wollte er mir zwar nicht geben, versprach aber, mich in meinem Hotel zu besuchen. Der Namen dieser Unterkunft wird mir immer im Gedächtnis bleiben. Es war das „Batik Palace Hotel" nahe dem Bahnhof von Yogyakarta. Wir trafen uns und es fiel mir wirklich schwer, meine Begeisterung nicht offen zu zeigen. Der Batik-Händler war aus Semarang, einem Ort nicht weit entfernt von der Stadt Pekalongan, die den Beinamen „Kota-Batik" trägt – Batik-Stadt. Mein neuer Bekannter klärte mich gerne und kenntnisreich über die lange indo-europäische Batik-

Tradition in Pekalongan auf. Als er mich verließ, war ich zwar um einige tausend Rupiah ärmer, dafür aber um viele Informationen reicher. Und vor allen Dingen: Ich war der stolze und neue Besitzer von zwei herrlichen Batiken, welche die Signaturen „E van Zuylen" beziehungsweise „L. Metz Pekalongan" trugen!

Ich hatte nun zwei schöne Souvenirs an das Gespräch mit dem auskunftsfreudigen Batik-Informanten – so dachte ich jedenfalls. Tatsächlich jedoch bildeten die beiden Batiken das Fundament meiner historischen Batik-Sammlung: Jeder, dem ich meine neuen alten Schätzchen zeigte, war beeindruckt, und ich fühlte mich bestärkt und beflügelt, nun intensiver nach Vergleichbarem zu suchen. Ich kannte ja jetzt zwei neue Schlüssel-Worte: „van Zuylen" und „Metzelaar". So war es im Grunde reiner Zufall gewesen, dass ich diese schöne neue Welt für mich entdeckt hatte. Die beiden Stücke haben mich bis heute begleitet (Abbildungen im Katalog Nr. 44 und Nr. 48, Anm. d. Red.)

Ardiyanto und ich sind nach wie vor gute Freunde. Damals bat er im Gegenzug für die Batiken, die er mir „in Kommission" übergab, um Kunstbücher aus Europa für sich. Heute besitzt er eine bedeutende Bibliothek und ist im Batik-Geschäft international erfolgreich.

Welche weiteren Ereignisse, Erlebnisse und Bekanntschaften haben Ihre spätere intensive Sammeltätigkeit und Ihre Beschäftigung mit historischen Batiken geprägt?

Zurück in Köln ging ich auf die Suche nach Literatur und stieß auf das holländische Buch von Alit Veldhuisen-Djajasoebrata „Batik op Java" von 1973. Alit war die Kuratorin für Indonesien am Völkerkunde-Museum in Rotterdam und es war lediglich ein Brief an sie nötig, um mir die beeindruckende Batiksammlung im Depot ansehen zu dürfen. Später lud Alit mich zu sich nach Hause ein, wo ich auch ihren Mann Harmen Veldhuisen kennenlernte. Mit beiden verbindet mich bis heute eine herzliche Freundschaft. Meine Fach-Bibliothek wuchs allmählich.

Dann fand 1985 im Kölner Rautenstrauch-Joest-Museum für Völkerkunde das Internationale Symposium zum Thema „Indonesian Textiles" statt. Hier kamen die Experten zusammen, deren Namen ich bisher nur aus Büchern kannte: Ruth Barnes, Mattiebelle Gittinger, Rens Heringa, Robert J.

Holmgren und Anita E. Spertus, Robyn J. Maxwell, Marie-Louise Nabholz-Kartaschoff, Urs Ramseyer, Shinobu Yoshimoto, Rita Bolland, Michael J. Hitchcock, Mary H. Kahlenberg u.a. – an dieser Veranstaltung musste ich natürlich unbedingt teilnehmen.

Als Trudel Klefisch (Inhaberin des Auktionshauses Klefisch, Köln; Anm. d. Red.) im Rahmen dieses Symposiums nach geeigneten Räumen für eine Auktion in der Nähe des Museums suchte, bot ich ihr daher gerne unsere Galerie-Räume an. Es war eine der ersten Auktionen indonesischer Textilien in Deutschland und alle jene berühmten und so freundlichen Experten kamen zu uns in die Galerie. Die Preise damals waren in der Tat sehr moderat, zumindest verglichen mit den Preisen, die heute auf Messen und Auktionen erzielt werden. Ich selbst ersteigerte damals die Batik mit dem Text „SLAMET NJANG PAKE" („Glück / Segen der Trägerin / dem Besitzer", Abbildung im Katalog Nr. 37; Anm. d. Red.).

**Zu den wichtigen Freundschaften, die sich aus dem Interesse an historischen Batiken ergaben, zählt auch Ihre Freundschaft mit Donald Harper.
Mr. Harper: Sie haben – wie Rudolf Smend, in den 1970er Jahren mit dem Sammeln von Batiken begonnen und bezeichneten es als ganz logisch, dass Sie beide sich einmal begegnen würden. Können Sie sich noch an Ihre erste Begegnung mit Rudolf Smend erinnern?**

Rudolf und ich lernten uns über einen gemeinsamen Freund kennen, der ebenfalls Batiken sammelte. Da wir beide großes Interesse an diesen Textilien hatten, verstanden wir uns auf Anhieb, und in den letzten 30 Jahren wurde unsere Freundschaft immer enger.

Im Gegensatz zu Rudolf Smend haben Sie Ihren Wohnsitz nach Java verlegt. Was hat Sie dazu bewogen, Ihr Leben hier zu verbringen?

Mitte der Siebziger Jahre reiste ich zum ersten Mal nach Indonesien. Seitdem habe ich meinen Wohnsitz in Yogyakarta. Anfangs zog mich das außerordentlich reiche kulturelle Leben Zentraljavas an. Im Laufe der Zeit interessierte ich mich jedoch ganz besonders für antike Batiken, und die konnte man am besten in Yogya sammeln. Hier fand man nicht nur Batiken aus ganz Java: Es war dies auch der einzige Ort, an dem man die qualitätvollsten zentral-

javanischen Arbeiten beziehen konnte, wie beispielsweise solche, die in den Kratons hergestellt wurden. Alte Batiken von den Fürstenhöfen Yogya und Solo gehören zu den besten, die jemals gemacht wurden. Sie sind so selten wie die seltensten Batiken der Nordküste. Außerhalb Zentraljavas sind sie allerdings beinahe unmöglich zu finden: Im Gegensatz zu Batiken der Nordküste, die in andere Teile Indonesiens „exportiert" wurden, konnte man die Stücke aus dem Kraton nur an der Quelle finden.

Rudolf Smends anfängliche Beschäftigung mit Batik zielte darauf ab, mit einer Galerie in Deutschland Kunst und Mentalität Javas beziehungsweise Indonesiens sowie die Techniken des Batikens zu vermitteln. Was waren Ihre Beweggründe, sich mit Batiken zu beschäftigen?

Ich bin mir eigentlich nicht sicher, warum mich die Batik anfänglich reizte. Im Nachhinein betrachtet, war es vielleicht einfach mein Schicksal, passionierter Sammler zu werden. Als mein Wissen über die Batik zunahm, wurde mir nach und nach klar, dass dieser Bereich der Textilkunst wegen seiner enormen Vielfalt an Stilrichtungen und Motiven ganz einzigartig war. Ich habe auch ein großes Interesse an anderen traditionellen indonesischen Textilien, doch bieten diese nicht die Vielfalt der Batik. Nach 30 Jahren Sammlertätigkeit langweilt das Thema mich also keineswegs, sondern ich entdecke noch immer Neues in der traditionellen Batik. Nach wie vor fasziniert sie mich sehr.

Herr Smend: Sie reisten zunächst noch häufig nach Indonesien, um dort neue Batiken für sich zu entdecken, bauten aber zugleich recht rasch Ihre Kontakte zu Fachleuten und Museen hier in Deutschland, insbesondere im Rheinland aus.

Das ist richtig – und was meine guten Verbindungen zum Textilmuseum in Krefeld betrifft, ließ sich sogar beides miteinander vereinen. Der Kontakt zum Textilmuseum kam über die erwähnte „Tournee" durch die Filialen der Dresdner Bank mit meinen Batik-Bildern zustande. Auch die Filiale in Krefeld hatte 1976 Interesse an einer Internationalen Batik-Ausstellung gezeigt. Bei der Eröffnung war das Haus voller lokaler Prominenz. Den Festvortrag hielt die damalige Direktorin des Krefelder Textilmuseums, Dr. Brigitte Menzel: eine kenntnisreiche und viel beachtete Einführung in die Geschichte der Batik, speziell in Krefeld. Bis zu

jenem Tage war mir die Bedeutung von Thorn Prikker für Krefeld überhaupt nicht klar gewesen. Auch von der Batik-Ausstellung vor genau 70 Jahren – 1906 – im Kaiser Wilhelm Museum, hörte ich bei dieser Gelegenheit zum ersten Mal.

Zu dem Textilmuseum – zu dieser Zeit noch am Frankenring – hatte ich seitdem eine freundschaftliche Verbindung. Durch den Umzug nach Krefeld-Linn und unter dem neuen Direktor, Carl-Wolfgang Schümann, gewann das Museum später sehr an internationaler Reputation.

Dr. Schümann reiste mit mir 1980 drei Wochen lang durch Java und Bali und war dort mein kenntnisreicher und hoch gebildeter Lehrer, dem ich viel zu verdanken habe. Er öffnete mir die Augen für kulturgeschichtliche, architektonische und kunsthandwerkliche Eigenheiten und Zusammenhänge und lenkte meinen etwas einseitig auf Batiken ausgerichteten Blick auch auf andere Textilien. Zusammen erwarben wir in jener Zeit eine stattliche und vorzeigbare Sammlung indonesischer Textilien für das Museum. Aus heutiger Sicht weiß ich, dass es wohl die letzte Möglichkeit war, mit so wenig Geld eine so exquisite Sammlung vor Ort zu erwerben.

Begannen Sie denn unter dem Eindruck dieser Reise Ihre Sammeltätigkeit auch auf andere Textilien auszuweiten?

Nein – aber es stimmt, dass diese Reise für meine Entwicklung als Sammler von Bedeutung war, denn ich musste mich nun bewusst entscheiden: Man kann nicht Batiken und die Textilien der anderen Inseln gleichzeitig sammeln. Entweder oder, wenn überhaupt. Der Trend der Sammler ging eindeutig zu den anderen Textilien. Batik wurde stets belächelt – „Das ist nur etwas für Frauen", oder „Die sehen doch langweilig aus" oder „Das ist ja in einer Manufaktur hergestellt worden" – das waren Sätze, die ich mir oft anhören musste. Aber ich war eigensinnig und fühlte mich wohl auf meinem Sammelgebiet: bei den Batik-Künstlerinnen und Künstlern, bei den Frauen auf dem Markt mit ihren Stapeln an Second Hand Batiken, in den Manufakturen, wo es nach Wachs roch und wo junge Mädchen und ältere Frauen bei mäßiger Beleuchtung mit großer Geduld und höchstem Geschick mit dem Canting auf dem Stoff zeichneten. Java, das war meine Welt. Nicht Bali und nicht Sumba oder Flores. Ich blieb bei meiner Linie, weil die Batiken keineswegs langweilig sind und dementsprechend auch das Sammeln dieser Textilien niemals langwei-

lig werden kann – da bin ich ganz einer Meinung mit Don Harper. Die Herstellung ist immer wieder spannend, das Färben eine große Kunst und es liegt stets eine ausgelassene und doch friedliche Stimmung über dem Ganzen. Es war für mich immer aufs Neue erstaunlich, wie schön die Produkte sind, wenn man sich die recht bescheidenen Arbeitsbedingungen und die geringe Bezahlung vergegenwärtigt.

Mr. Harper, Sie haben Rudolf Smend über die vielen Jahren hindurch bei der Erweiterung seiner Batiksammlung beraten und haben ihm Objekte vermittelt. Was machte für Sie die Zusammenarbeit mit Rudolf Smend so reizvoll? Was zeichnet seine heutige Sammlung aus Ihrer Sicht aus?

Der entscheidende Punkt für die nach so vielen Jahren noch immer erfolgreiche Zusammenarbeit mit Rudolf ist, dass sie immer problemlos verlief und ein Vergnügen war, weil er solch ein Gentleman ist. Rudolfs Sammlung ist deshalb so ausgezeichnet, weil er sich dem Batiksammeln ernsthaft widmete und sich von seinem Engagement niemals abbringen ließ – nicht einmal dann, als schöne Batiken weniger leicht zu haben waren und die Preise in die Höhe schnellten.

Sie beschäftigen sich neben Batiken auch intensiv mit anderen indonesischen Textilien, beispielsweise mit den so genannten Songkets – mit Gold durchwebten Stoffen.

Richtig, ich sammle nicht nur alte Batiken, sondern auch andere indonesische Textilien. Meine Sammlung alter Brokate aus Sumatra (Songkets) halte ich für etwas Besonderes, da ich seit vielen Jahren ziemlich regelmäßig ins südliche Sumatra und auf die Insel Bangka reise. Grundsätzlich würde ich sagen, dass die Songkets nach den Batiken meine zweitliebsten indonesischen Textilien sind. Ich finde, auch die Songkets bieten viele verschiedene Stilrichtungen, die nur von Batiken übertroffen werden. Ein weiterer „Vorteil" der Songkets ist, dass die heutigen Weber in Palembang noch immer sehr schöne Exemplare herstellen und dass dieses Gewerbe blüht...

151

In welchem Umfang findet man heute auf Java noch traditionelle Batikherstellung?

Mir scheint, die traditionelle Batikindustrie ist rückläufig. Soweit ich weiß, fertigen heute nur noch wenige Menschen traditionelle Batiken von sehr guter Qualität, weil die Nachfrage so gering ist. Die Nachfrage nach hochwertigen neuen Songkets jedoch ist noch genauso hoch wie immer, obwohl diese Arbeiten sehr teuer sind. Nur noch ganz Wenige wenden hohe Summen für Batikarbeiten auf, obwohl zur Blütezeit der Batikproduktion die wirklich guten Stücke ebenfalls ziemlich teuer waren. Damit ein Gewerbe lebendig und vital bleibt, muss natürlich ein echter Bedarf für die Produkte bestehen. In der Vergangenheit waren hochwertige Batiken sehr gefragt, da die meisten Menschen eine gute Arbeit sehr wohl von einer schlechten unterscheiden konnten. Mit dem Aufkommen billiger, unechter „Batiken" aus Siebdruckproduktion und dem ständigen Wandel der Kultur Javas ist dies nicht mehr der Fall. Für diejenigen, die heute noch schöne, traditionelle Batiken herstellen, ist die Fertigung daher nicht mehr sehr lukrativ. Schöne Batiken waren früher in den Palästen und in den Gemeinden reicher Araber und Peranakan-Chinesen gefragt. Mit dem Wandel dieser Kulturen veränderte sich jedoch auch die Batikindustrie. Wenn die meisten Verbraucher kaum noch in der Lage sind, eine gute Batik von einer minderwertigen zu unterscheiden, dann ist es nur verständlich, dass sie keinen Aufpreis für erstklassige Stücke zahlen, und so leidet das Gewerbe. Es ist unmöglich, ohne großen Zeitaufwand und ein hohes Maß an Fachkönnen, Batiken von wirklich schöner Qualität herzustellen.

Dagegen ist zum Glück die Nachfrage nach hochwertigen traditionellen Textilien in Sumatra noch sehr groß, und die Webergemeinde von Palembang liegt noch immer im Wettstreit um die Fertigung der besten Songkets. Es ist großartig, dass ein solches Gewerbe im 21. Jahrhundert noch floriert. Die meisten Träger von Songkets sind sehr anspruchsvoll und gern bereit, die Weber sehr gut für Unikate zu bezahlen, die sie mit Stolz tragen können und um die andere sie beneiden. Es geht immer um den Status und den guten Geschmack, aber die wirtschaftliche Seite ist eben auch ein wichtiger Faktor.
Leider scheint es mir, als ob diese Dynamik im traditionellen Batikgewerbe nicht mehr existiert, und *ich vermute, dass die Batikherstellung letzten Endes zu einem Kunsthandwerk von vielen wird und seinen einstmals hohen Status nicht behält. Sammlungen wie die von Rudolf Smend versetzen uns in die glückliche Lage, die wirklich fantastische frühere Schönheit traditioneller Batiken zu sehen.*

Herr Smend, nun haben Sie eine umfangreiche, einzigartige Sammlung zusammen getragen – trennen Sie sich auch schon einmal von einem Ihrer Objekte?

Die Sammlung zeigt meine Vorlieben, auch wenn sie sehr breit angelegt ist. Sicher stand die Qualität bei der Sammeltätigkeit mit im Vordergrund, aber durch den weitgehenden Verzicht auf Spezialisierung gibt die Sammlung nun einen guten Überblick zur motivischen Vielfalt.
Natürlich hängt man an jedem einzelnen Objekt... Mit vielen sind ja ganz persönliche Erinnerungen oder Erwerbsgeschichten verbunden. Zum Beispiel ein Kemben (siehe „Batiken von Fürstenhöfen und Sultanspalästen", Köln 2000, S. 27, Nr. 12; Anm. d. Red.) – Ich hatte ihn vor Jahren von T.T. Soerjanto erhalten, die mir damals Unterricht in der Batiktechnik erteilte. Der Kemben stammt aus dem Kraton, dem Sultanspalast von Yogyakarta, zu dem sie gute Kontakte hatte. Heute leitet T.T. Soerjanto das Danar Hadi Batik-Museum in Solo und hat wesentlich an der Publikation „Batik – The Impact of Time and Environment" mitgewirkt. 1984, hatte ich ihr einen Gefallen getan, für den sie sich mit zwei Kemben revanchierte: Ihrem Mann, einem leidenschaftlichen Jäger, wollte sie ein deutsches Markengewehr schenken. Ich sollte es im Flugzeug mitbringen, natürlich ganz offiziell. Wie fast immer, wenn man etwas wirklich will, klappte das ohne allzu große Probleme und in Yogyakarta tauschten wir dann die Objekte der Begierde (zweiter Kemben siehe Nr. 14 in diesem Buch; Anm. d. Red.).
Das erste Mal, dass ich mich von Batiken aus meiner Sammlung trennte, ist noch gar nicht so lange her. Im Jahr 2005 wurde der Grundstein für das neue Rautenstrauch-Joest-Museum im Zentrum von Köln gelegt. Aus diesem Anlass machte der Sammler und Hobby-Ethnologe Dr. Borwin Lüth, Hannover, dem Museum eine Schenkung: Die Kuratorin, Brigitte Khan Majlis, sollte sich aus meiner Sammlung einige Batiken aussuchen, die dann zur Einweihung des Museums an prominenter Stelle ausgestellt würden. Da ich die Textilien gleichzeitig in besten

Händen wusste, fiel mir die Trennung nicht so ungeheuer schwer. Auf die Stücke war Brigitte Khan Majlis übrigens durch den Katalog „Batiken von Fürstenhöfen und Sultanspalästen" (2000) aufmerksam geworden, an dessen Entstehung sie aktiv beteiligt gewesen war. Mit diesem Schritt war der Damm nun sozusagen gebrochen und ich hatte das getan, wovor mich Dr. Schümann stets gewarnt hatte.

Kürzlich bekam ich eine Anfrage von dem Peranakan-Museum in Singapore bezüglich der Batik, die chinesische Spielkarten darstellt (Nr. 45 in diesem Katalog; Anm. d. Red.). Dieses Stück würde natürlich sehr gut in das dortige exquisite Museum passen. Die Batik hatte früher Brian Brake gehört, dem bedeutenden Photographen aus Auckland. Nach seinem Tode hatte es Don Harper 1990 bei Christie's ersteigert und dann habe ich es von ihm erworben. Sicher wäre es auch in seinem Sinne, wenn es jetzt in das Singapore Museum kommt.

Köln, im Juli 2006
(Interview: Sabine Philipp)

Interview with Rudolf G. Smend and Donald J. Harper

Mr Smend, your first visit to Indonesia, the home of batik, wasn't really planned at all...

At the time, in 1972, my girlfriend and I were actually planning to emigrate to Australia. We had covered the entire distance by car and crossed many countries – when the entry requirements for Australia changed at short notice. The closer we got to our actual destination, the less attractive it seemed to us – we didn't hear many positive things about the country from the emigrants we met. But people kept praising Indonesia. When we arrived there, we found this information confirmed. The people were so friendly, open and spontaneous, life was inexpensive and the climate was good. After the Soekarno era, it was an euphoric time of new departures in Yogyakarta, with the economy picking up somewhat and tourism just starting. We therefore spontaneously changed our travel destination and stayed in Indonesia.

When did you first become aware of batiks?

It was in Yogyakarta, Java. We had heard that this city was the batik centre of Indonesia. Curious and always open to cultural experiences, we visited the sultan's so-called water castle where we were told a number of "batik galleries" had recently opened. They exhibited the newly discovered "batik paintings", pictorial textiles that were in the surrealist style, for example, but made in the traditional batik technique. We became friends with Gianto, one of these batik artists, and during the course of a week he taught us how to handle the canting, using wax and both lightfast and colourfast dyes in powder form. To our great surprise the latter had been made in Germany... For our friend, we soon turned into an attraction that was good for business: two Germans sitting on small stools, attempting to learn the batik technique – Indeed... once we gained an insight into the technique we truly learned to appreciate the skill involved and the artistic merit of these indigenous products. The prices asked for them seemed incredibly reasonable to us. Because Gianto refused to accept money for his lessons, we purchased a number of his paintings before we left.

But that was still a long way from wanting to collect historic batiks...

Yes, of course. It was much later when I actively began to collect antique batik textiles – by way of our idea of opening a batik gallery in Germany. And this idea grew during our later journey, when we stayed in Bali. There we decorated our meagre accommodation with Gianto's batik paintings – it was almost beginning to look like a batik gallery. Realising the great response from our European house mates, we promoted Gianto and his work, and explained the technique inasmuch as we had been able to understand it ourselves. Yes, I believe, this was where the idea was born to open a kind of batik gallery in Cologne, a tea house – which were "in" at the time – where we could pass on some of the hospitality we had ourselves experienced on the trip, where one could feel at home... By now, the idea of emigrating to Australia had lost its appeal, our Indonesian visa was due to expire – and we were in fact a little homesick... On our return to Java we put together a collection of 50 batik paintings. Because our budget was limited, we had to choose with great care and become well informed. We visited every important batik producer and found out details about the batik tradition at the State Batik Research Institute. Finally we returned to Germany with a fine supply of modern and traditional batiks in a large variety of sizes and designs.

Rudolf shows his new aquisition: snowwhite and
the dwarfs. Intern. Batik Exhibition. Hagen, 1980.

Rudolf and Donald with Ibu Nus and her sisters showing batik
to German batik artists in Kirana Guesthouse. Yogyakarta, 1985

Rudolf with Pak Hadjir, Harjiman Mashar, Alfons Haryadi
and An Sujanto. Yogyakarta, 1985

The batik gallery was quite obviously a success, as it became the starting point for your textile gallery today...

Yes, if one considers that our batik gallery in 1973 wasn't based on any amazing business idea... But to our own surprise, it became really successful. There were mostly friends and acquaintances at the opening – we had much to talk about after all... We previously advertised the event in every café and pub in the south of Cologne. In retrospect, it has to be said that the idea for a "batik gallery" came at exactly the right time. It tied in with a sense of longing, a kind of hope with regard to everything that originated "in the East". India, in particular, was considered to be a source of healing. We only need to think back to the photos of the Beatles with their guru, to the legendary "Concert for Bangladesh" and the Sanyassins, who lived in the Ashram in Poona and kept in close contact with their master Baghwan.

Here in Cologne, the now legendary Harry Owens started a flea market in 1972, and the idea soon spread to Düsseldorf, Bonn and Aachen. For a "start-up business" like our completely unknown batik gallery, these flea markets were the ideal venue. They attracted visitors from every level of society, and it was possible to try not only one's products but also test oneself. However, at the time I was simply concerned with making money from my sole piece of capital – the 50 batik paintings brought with me in my rucksack – I was totally convinced of their value.

How were batik textiles rated in Germany at the time – what was the response to your particular passion, your "business idea"?

The response, as it were, was mixed. Personally I was so confident of the status of batik art that I applied to exhibit at the Internationale Kunst Markt (IKM), the art fair that Ingo Kümmel founded in Düsseldorf in 1973, as a kind of protest fair against the Cologne Art Fair where he and his gallery collection had not been accepted. He was able to get the support of many top galleries for his project, and I found myself exhibiting next to the stand of the Swiss Krugier Gallery which deals in high quality works of art. Krugier, however, thought their proximity to Indonesian batik motifs of cock fights and Ramayana rather less appropriate. They collected signatures to stop the Batik Gallery participating at future fairs. This did at least get us plenty of attention, and the North-Rhine-Westphalia TV-station featured our rather colourful batiks. Fortunately, all this fuss also brought us a few buyers, so overall the fair was a success for me after all. I did in fact exhibit at the fair again in 1974, but not next to Krugier...

At the same art fair I was discovered by a visitor who made batiks herself. Until that time I had no idea this "art form" was being taught in Germany and that there had been a "batik movement" during the time of the Emperor as well as another one after the Second World War. The husband of this visitor and batik expert was then a board member of the Dresdner Bank in Cologne. Perhaps it was due to her "helper syndrome" or perhaps due to her love for batik, in any case, she put me, with my somewhat different agenda, in touch with the PR

155

department of the Dresdner Bank in Cologne. The bank expressed great enthusiasm for the exotic batiks, which seemed to be perfectly suited for display in the main halls of the bank's branches. It was a learning experience for me, how to organise private views, how to do PR work, and what invitations and leaflets need to look like, always making very sure that the address of the gallery was highly visible.

On the whole these events encouraged me in my idea for a batik gallery, and I travelled again to Java in order to visit artists and purchase suitable batik paintings for my gallery collection.

Was there a key moment that you could describe as the starting point for your interest in historic batiks and your desire to collect them?

Yes, I first became keenly aware of historic batiks through my contact with Ardiyanto, a Chinese man who had been one of my favourite suppliers of batiks since 1973.

During one of my visits – in 1976 – I happened to be present when a dealer showed him antique batiks, which Ardiyanto examined with an expert eye but did not buy in the end. The conversation took place in Indonesian, of course. I didn't understand much, but quickly realised that these batiks were particularly beautiful. I had never seen anything like it before – I had no idea that such textiles existed. One only saw ordinary batiks on the streets and in the markets, and not those made for the "upper class". I was so impressed by the dealer's wonderful fabrics that I requested his name and address. He was reluctant to give these to me but promised to pay me a visit at my hotel. I will always remember the name of the place. It was the "Batik Palace Hotel" near the Yogyakarta station.

We met and I found it extremely hard to hide my enthusiasm. The batik dealer came from Semarang, a place not far from the town of Pekalongan, which has the sobriquet "Kota-Batik" - Batik Town. My new acquaintance was happy to pass on his considerable knowledge of the long-standing Indo-European batik tradition in Pekalongan. When he left, I may have been a few thousand rupiah poorer, but considerably richer in information. And above all, I was the proud new owner of two magnificent batiks, with the inscribed initials "E van Zuylen" and "L. Metz Pekalongan", respectively!

I now had two beautiful souvenirs of my conversation with this knowledgeable batik informant – or so I thought. The two batiks, however, did become the foundation of my collection of historic batiks. Everyone to whom I showed my new ancient treasures was impressed, and I felt assured and inspired by this experience to concentrate on searching for similar pieces. I did, after all, know two new key words: "van Zuylen" and "Metzelaar". So, it was pure chance that I discovered this beautiful new world for myself. Both pieces are still with me today. (Catalogue illustration nos. 44 and 48, ed.)

Ardiyanto and I have remained good friends. At the time he asked me for art books "as commission" for the batiks. Today he has a substantial library and is internationally successful in the batik business.

Which other events, experiences and people later shaped your focussed collecting activity and your involvement with historic batiks?

On my return to Cologne, I started researching specialist literature and came across the Dutch book "Batik op Java" by Alit Veldhuisen-Djajasoebrata from 1973. Alit was curator of the Indonesian department at the Rotterdam Ethnology Museum, and it took no more than a letter to her to gain admission to the impressive batik collection in the museum depot. I was subsequently invited by Alit to her home where I also met her husband, Harmen Veldhuisen. I have stayed close friends with both until today. My specialist library began to expand.

In 1985, the Cologne Rautenstrauch Joest Museum of Ethnology hosted the International Symposium on "Indonesian Textiles". This brought together experts whose names I had previously only known from books: Ruth Barnes, Mattiebelle Gittinger, Rens Heringa, Robert J. Holmgren and Anita E. Spertus, Robyn J. Maxwell, Marie-Louise Nabholz-

Kartaschoff, Urs Ramseyer, Shinobu Yoshimoto, Rita Bolland, Michael J. Hitchcock, Mary H. Kahlenberg, etc. – Of course, I absolutely had to participate in this event.

When Trudel Klefisch (owner of Klefisch auctioneers, Cologne; ed.) was looking for suitable premises near the museum for an auction accompanying the symposium, I was pleased to offer our gallery space. It was one of the first auctions of Indonesian textiles in Germany and all these famous and so very friendly experts came to our gallery. The prices then really were very modest, at least compared with prices achieved at fairs and auctions today. Personally I bought a batik with the inscription "SLAMET NJANG PAKE" ("Luck / blessing for the owner / wearer", catalogue plate no. 37; ed.).

Your friendship with Don Harper started through your interest for historical batiks.
Mr Don Harper: Like Rudolf Smend you began collecting batik in the 1970s, and indicated that it would be quite logical for the two of you to meet one day. Can you still remember your first encounter with Rudolf Smend?

Rudolf and I were first introduced by a mutual friend who also collected batik. Since we were both keenly interested in such textiles, we hit it off right away and our friendship has flourished over the past 30 years.

Unlike Rudolf Smend you took up residence in Java. What induced you to spend your life there?

I first travelled to Indonesia in the mid-seventies and have been based in Yogyakarta ever since. Initially, I was attracted to the extraordinarily rich cultural life in Central Java but as time passed, I became particularly interested in antique batiks and Jogja was the best place to collect them. Not only could one find batiks from all over Java there, it was the only place to source the best quality Central Javanese pieces such as those made in the kratons. Old pieces from the courts of Yogya and Solo were some of the best batiks ever made. They are as rare as the rarest Northcoast batiks but are almost impossible to find outside of Central Java. Unlike Northcoast batiks that were "exported" to other parts of Indonesia, the kraton pieces could only be found at the source.

Rudolf Smend's initial purpose in engaging with batik was to convey the art and mentality of Java/Indonesia, and their batik techniques, to the German public through a gallery.
What was your motivation for engaging with batik?

I am not sure just why I was initially attracted to batik. In retrospect, I suppose it was just my fate to become an avid collector. As my knowledge of batik increased, I slowly discovered that this area of textile art was very unique because of the enormous variety of styles and motifs. I am also very interested in other kinds of traditional Indonesia textiles, but none of them offer the variety that batik does. So after 30 years, instead of being bored with the subject, I am still discovering new things about traditional batik and am still quite fascinated by it.

Mr Smend, initially you travelled many times to Indonesia to discover new batiks for yourself, but you also quickly established contacts with specialists and museums in Germany, in particular in the Rhineland.

That's correct – and as far as my good connections with the textile museum in Krefeld were concerned, it became possible to combine the two. My contact with the Textile Museum was a result of the above-mentioned "exhibition tour" of my batik paintings at branches of the Dresdner Bank. The branch in Krefeld also showed an interest in an international batik exhibition, and at the opening the place was full of local VIPs. The then director of the Krefeld Textile Museum, Dr Brigitte Menzel, gave the opening lecture, a well-informed and much noted introduction to the history of batik, with particular reference to Krefeld. Until that day I had been completely unaware how important Thorn Prikker had been for Krefeld, and it was the first time I heard about the batik exhibition at the Kaiser Wilhelm Museum exactly 70 years previously. I have been in friendly contact with the museum ever since. At the time it was still located at the Frankenring, and after moving to Krefeld-Linn, under the guidance of the new director, Carl-Wolfgang Schümann, the museum significantly heightened its international renown.

In 1980, I went on a three-week tour of Java and Bali with Dr Schümann, who became my knowledgeable and highly educated mentor to whom I owe a great deal. He opened my eyes to cultural, historical, architectural and craft features and contexts and directed my somewhat one-sided, batik-fixated attention to other textiles. Together we acquired a superb, presentable collection of Indonesian textiles for the museum. Looking back I am aware that this would probably have been the last time when it was possible to acquire such an exquisite collection at such a low cost in situ.

In view of the impression this trip left on you, did you start collecting other textiles?

No - but it is true that this trip was important for my development as a collector, insofar as I had to make a conscious decision. It wasn't possible to collect both batiks and the textiles from the other islands at the same time. Either or, if at all. Collectors clearly tended to favour other textiles. Batiks were always looked down on – "They are for women" or "They look boring" or "This has been made in a craftshop" – such were the remarks I frequently had to listen to. But I was persistent and as a collector I was happy in my field: among the batik artists, among the women in the markets with their piles of second-hand batiks and in the dimly-lit workshops smelling of wax, where young girls and older women employed the canting to draw on fabrics with great patience and exceptional skill. Java was my world. Not Bali, nor Sumba or Flores. I remained true to my interest because batiks are by no means boring and therefore collecting them can never become boring either – I quite agree with Don Harper in this respect. The production is always exciting, the dyeing process is a great art, and it is always done in a cheerful but peaceful atmosphere. I was always surprised anew how beautiful these textiles are, considering the relatively modest working conditions and low pay.

Mr Harper: In all those years you also acted as adviser to Rudolf Smend regarding expansion of his batik collection. You arranged for him to purchase objects and were something of a consultant to him. What made working with Rudolf Smend so attractive to you? In your view, what distinguishes the current Rudolf Smend collection?

The key thing about successfully working with Rudolf after so many years was that he made it easy and fun to do so because he is such a gentleman. Rudolf's collection is an excellent one because he made a serious commitment to focus on collecting batik and never wavered in his commitment even as the availability of fine batik decreased and prices skyrocketed.

You are collecting batiks like Rudolf Smend but you are also studying brocades woven with gold thread, the so-called songkets?

Indeed, I also collect old batik as well as other kinds of Indonesian textiles. I believe my collection of old Sumatran brocades (songkets) is a special one because I have been travelling to Southern Sumatra and the island of Bangka quite regularly for many years. Generally speaking, after batik, my second favorite textile in Indonesia is songket. I think songkets also offer an array of styles only surpassed by batik. Another good thing about songket is that the present day weavers in Palembang are still making extremely fine examples and the industry is thriving.

To what extent is traditional batik production still found in Java today?

The traditional batik industry, to me, seems to be on the decline. As far as I know, there are very few people making great quality traditional batik today because the demand is so small. However, the demand for high quality new songkets is as strong as ever even though such pieces are quite expensive. Very few people will spend a big sum for a batik anymore even though back in the heyday of batik production, great pieces were quite expensive. Naturally, in order to keep an industry alive and vital, there has to be a genuine need for what it produces. In the past, there was a strong demand for high quality batik because most people could easily recognise a good piece from a poor one. However, with the advent of cheap, silk-screened

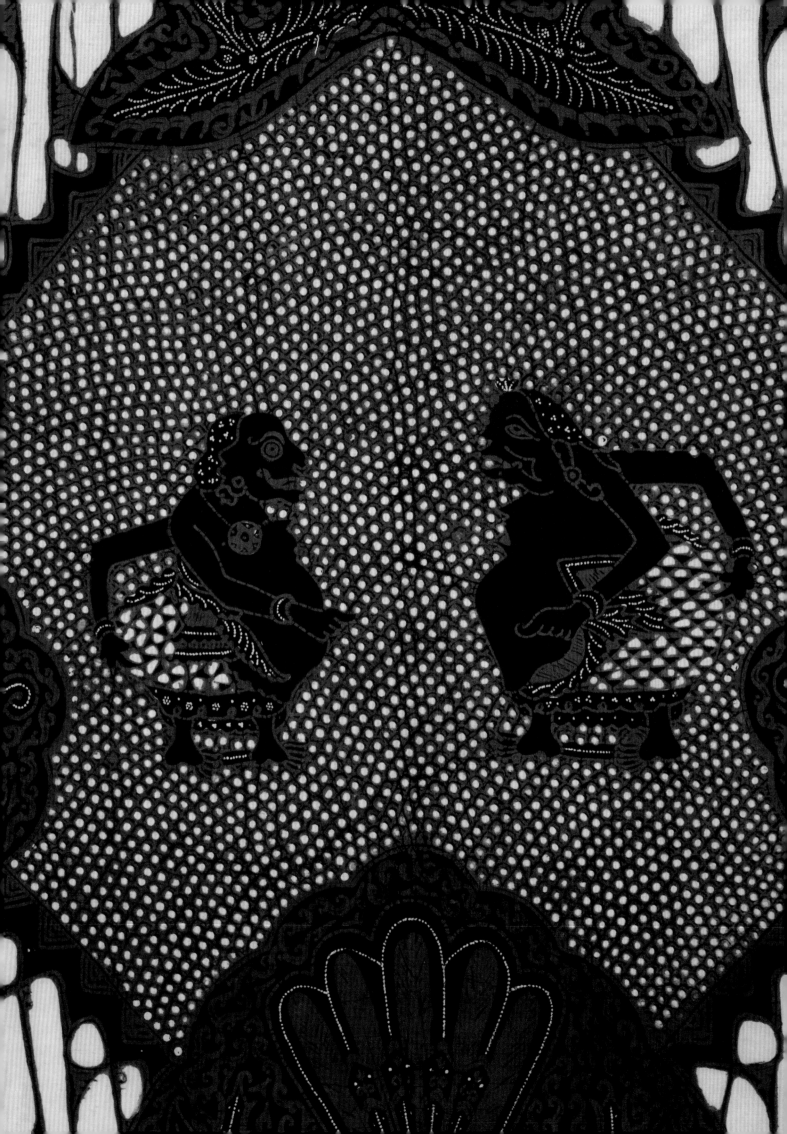

fake "batiks", and the ever-changing culture of Java, that is no longer the case. Consequently, it is not very lucrative now for those who are still making fine traditional batik. The demand for fine batik used to come from the palaces and communities of the rich "peranakan" Chinese and Arabs. But as those cultures changed, so did the batik industry. If most consumers are hardly able to recognise a good batik from an inferior one, it only stands to reason that they will not pay a premium to get a high quality piece and so the industry suffers. It is impossible to make a truly fine quality batik without expending a lot of time and a great deal of skill.

Fortunately, in Sumatra the demand for high quality traditional textiles is still very strong and the community of weavers in Palembang are, to this day, keenly competing with one another to make the best songkets. It's great to see such an industry still thriving in the 21st century. Most people who wear songkets have very high standards and will eagerly pay the weavers very well to acquire one-of-a-kind pieces that they will be proud to wear and others will admire. It's all about status and good taste but economics are also big factor.

Alas, it seems to me those dynamics hardly exist in the traditional batik industry anymore so I suspect that batik-making may eventually become just another handicraft and will not be able to retain the high status it once had. However, with collections like the Rudolf Smend one, we are fortunate to be able to see how truly fantastic traditional batik once was.

Mr Smend, having put together a comprehensive, unique collection, do you ever part with one of your pieces?

The collection illustrates my preferences even if it is very broad in its scope. Quality was, of course, one of the top collection criteria, but by largely avoiding specialisation, the collection now provides a good overview of the diversity of motifs.

I am naturally attached to each individual piece... Many of them hold personal memories or stories to do with their acquisition. For example the kemben (see "Batik from the courts of Java and Sumatra", p. 23, no. 12; ed.) which I received several years ago from T.T. Soerjanto, who was teaching me the batik

technique at the time. This kemben came from the kraton, the sultan's palace in Yogyakarta, to which she had good connections. Today T.T. Soerjanto is in charge of the Danar Hadi Batik-Museum in Solo and is a major contributor to the publication, "Batik – The Impact of Time and Environment". In 1984 I did her a favour and she paid me back with two kemben. Her husband was an enthusiastic hunter and she wanted to give him a quality gun "Made in Germany". I was meant to take it on the plane, completely legally of course. And as almost always if you really want something, it worked out without too many problems, and in Yogyakarta we exchanged the objects of our hearts' desire (second kemben, see no. 14 in the catalogue; ed.).

The first time I parted with batiks from my collection is not so very long ago. In 2005, the foundation stone for the new Rautenstrauch-Joest-Museum was laid in the centre of Cologne. On this occasion the collector and amateur ethnologist, Dr Johann-Borwin Lüth from Hannover made a donation to the museum. The curator, Brigitte Khan Majlis, could select a number of batiks from my collection to be put on prominent display for the museum's inauguration. Because I knew my textiles to be in excellent hands, the separation was not too painful. Brigitte Khan Majlis had first come across the pieces during her active involvement in the production of the catalogue "Batiks from Courts and Palaces" (2000). This opened the floodgates and I did what Dr Schümann had always warned me about.

I recently received a request from the Peranakan Museum in Singapore regarding the batik depicting Chinese playing cards (no. 45 in this book; ed.) It would of course be a very fitting piece for that exquisite museum. The batik used to belong to the late New Zealand photographer, Brian Brake, and was bought after his death at Christie's by Don Harper in about 1990. Later I acquired it from Don. I'm sure that Brian would be happy were he to know that the piece eventually ended up in a Singapore museum.

Cologne, July 2006
(Interview by Sabine Philipp)

Glossar

Badan - der „Körper" eines Sarongs; er bildet den größeren Teil eines Sarongs. Der andere Teil wird als „Kopf" bezeichnet (siehe *kepala*)

Bang - rote Farbe, das verbindende Merkmal beinahe aller Batiken aus Nordjava

Bang-bangan - ausschließlich mit roter Farbe gefärbte Stoffe

Bangun tulak - schwarz-weiße *kemben*, die in den verletzlichsten Lebenssituationen wie Schwangerschaft oder Krankheit als Schutztuch verwendet werden

Batik - Reservefärbeverfahren, bei dem ein Reservemittel wie heißes Wachs oder Reispaste auf die Oberfläche von Stoffen aufgetragen wird, um diese Bereiche beim Färben auszusparen und ungefärbte Muster zu bilden. Nach dem Färben wird das Reservemittel durch Auskochen, Ausschmelzen oder Abkratzen entfernt

Batik cap - Batiktuch, bei dem der Wachsauftrag für die Musterung mit einem speziellen Metallstempel vorgenommen wird

Batik kaligrafi - für Sumatra produzierte Stoffe mit Zitaten aus dem Koran und Anrufungen Allahs in arabischer Schrift

Batik tulis - Batiktuch, dessen Muster mit dem *canting* gemalt sind (siehe *tulis*)

Buta - tropfenförmiges Motiv aus Indien, das bei der Ornamentierung von Kaschmir-Schals eine bedeutende Rolle spielt (siehe *lar*)

Buyr - einheitliche Ornamentierung bei den *kemben* für unverheiratete Frauen

Canting - javanischer Name für ein kleines Batikwerkzeug, bestehend aus einem Holz- oder Bambusgriff und einem Kupfergefäß mit einer oder mehreren Ausflusstüllen, durch die das flüssige Wachs kontrolliert auf die Stoffoberfläche aufgetragen werden kann

Cap - javanischer Begriff für einen meist aus Kupferblechstreifen konstruierten Metallstempel, mit dem beim Batikverfahren das flüssige Wachs auf die Stoffoberfläche aufgebracht wird. Ein cap bildet eine komplette Mustereinheit

celana - Batikhose, oft die Kleidung der chinesischen und europäischen Bewohner Javas

Cherki - Kartenspiel, südchinesischen Ursprungs, beliebt bei den Peranakan, in Singapur, Malacca und Penang, sowie in Indonesien, vor allem vor dem Zweiten Weltkrieg. Insbesondere bei den Frauen beliebter Zeitvertreib. Man spielte Zuhause, nicht nur im Alltag, sondern auch zu festlichen Anlässen, wie Geburtstagen, Neujahrsfeiern und gelegentlich auch bei Beerdigungen.

Ciptoning - *wayang*-Muster auf Batiktextilien

Dodot - langes Hüfttuch, etwa viermal so groß wie ein *sarong*, das früher Angehörige von Fürstenfamilien und der Aristokratie sowie Tänzer am Hof trugen. Es wurde auf verschiedenartige Weise um den Körper geschlungen

Garuda - mythischer Vogel; Reittier des Gottes Vishnu in der hinduistischen Mythologie

Iket kepala - Kopftuch für Männer, das bei förmlichen Anlässen auf verschiedenartige Weise zum Turban gebunden wurde

Indigo - *nilo*. Blauer Farbstoff, der aus Pflanzen der Arten Indigofera und Marsdenia gewonnen wird. Die Blätter reagieren mit einer alkalischen Lösung und bilden so ein aktives Präzipitat

Kain - „Tuch"; mit diesem Terminus werden generell flache, rechteckige Stoffe bezeichnet

Kain bang-biru - Batiken aus Nordjava in Blau und Rot, der häufigsten Farbkombination der *kain-laseman*-Stoffe

Kain kelengan - ausschließlich dunkelblau oder schwarz gefärbte Stoffe aus Nordjava; sie wurden als Trauerkleidung getragen

Kain kembangan - „geblümter Stoff". *Kemben*, bei dem die Batiktechnik mit anderen Reservefärbeverfahren wie *plangi* (Abbindetechnik) und *tritik* (Nähreservierung) kombiniert wurde

Kain laseman - Batiken aus den chinesischen Werkstätten von Lasem. Die Muster zeigen den Einfluss indischer Chintzstoffe sowie der chinesischen Ikonografie

Kain panjang - „Langtuch" oder Hüfttuch von ungefähr 250 cm Länge und 105-110 cm Breite für formellere Anlässe. Das ungenähte Tuch wird von Männern wie Frauen um die Hüften geschlungen und der letzte Teil meist vorn in eine Reihe von Falten gelegt, die beim Gehen fächerförmig auseinanderfallen

Kain sprei - Bettüberwurf

Kawung - berühmtes altes Motiv, bestehend aus zwei parallelen Reihen von Kreisen. Es existieren viele Variationen

Kebaya - loses Kleidungsstück aus weißem Kattun mit weiten Ärmeln, mit dem sich ursprünglich Frauen gemischter portugiesischer oder chinesischer Abstammung kleideten

Kemben - Brusttuch der Frau

Kepala - „Kopf" eines *sarong*, bestehend aus einem aufrecht stehenden Rechteck mit einer vom „Körper" (siehe *badan*) abweichenden Farbgebung und Musterung

TAN TJIE LAN · TIONG HOA

Kraton - Javanischer Palast in Yogyakarta und Surakarta auf Zentraljava

Kris - Dolch. Verkörpert den männlichen Aspekt des Universums. Bei der offiziellen Hofkleidung Zentraljavas werden Batikrock und kris stets zusammen getragen

Kudhung - rechteckiges Tuch, etwas breiter als ein *selendang*, das von muslimischen Frauen als Kopf- und Schultertuch getragen wird

Lar - Motiv, das einen einzelnen Flügel des Vogels Garuda darstellt. Es war für Personen von niedrigerem Rang an den javanischen Höfen bestimmt (siehe *buta*)

Larangan - Gruppe „verbotener" Motive. Ihre Verwendung war ab Ende des 18. Jahrhunderts dem Sultan und hohen Hofbeamten vorbehalten

Laseman - *kain laseman*

Latar putih - „weißer Hintergrund". Technik, bei der farbige Muster auf einem hellen, ungefärbten Hintergrund erscheinen. Eines der am schwersten auszuführenden Batikmuster unter den *kain laseman*

Mengkudu - einer der indonesischen Termini für den roten Farbstoff, welcher aus den Wurzeln der Morinda citrifolia gewonnen wird. Die daraus erzielte leuchtend rote Farbe ist auf den *pasisir* Batiken zu finden

Mui li (chines.) - Türvorhang, oft mit Batik verziert und bei Hochzeiten von Peranakan oder Chinesen über die Tür des Brautgemachs gehängt. Bei speziellen Zeremonien oder Anlässen wie z. B. dem Chinesischen Neujahr wurden sie auch überall im Hause über der Tür aufgehängt

Nilo - Indigo

Nitik - von den indischen *patola* auf die javanische Batik übertragenes Muster. Seine Ausführung in Wachs erfordert ein besonders konstruiertes *canting*

Pagi sore - Morgen / Spätnachmittag. Ein diagonal geteiltes Format mit einer vorwiegend hellen (Morgen) und einer vorwiegend dunklen Hälfte (Spätnachmittag), die jeweils entweder morgens oder abends getragen werden

Parang - berühmtes diagonales „Messermotiv", bestehend aus abwechselnd hellen und dunklen Streifen in Kontrastfarben mit wellenförmigem oder gebogtem Rand. Der Tradition nach war das Muster fürstlichen Personen vorbehalten

Two Javanese women and a baby, photo by Tan Tjie Lan. Batavia, c. 1900

Parang rusak - „zerbrochener Dolch". Motiv aus fortlaufenden Wellenbändern, die in diagonalen Reihen über die gesamte Stoffoberfläche verlaufen

Pasisir - Nordküste von Java

Patola - aus Indien gehandelte Textilien, die als luxuriöseste aller indischen Stoffe galten. Patola sind Seidenstoffe mit Ornamentierung in Doppel-ikat-Technik, deren Muster keine durchgehenden Linien aufweisen, sondern aus winzigen, quadrati-schen Einheiten aufgebaut sind (siehe *nitik)*

Peranakan - Jene Chinesen auf der indonesischen und malayischen Inselgruppe, deren Familien bereits seit mehreren Generationen dort gelebt haben (im Unterschied zu den „totoks", die erst kürzlich aus Festland-China eingewandert sind)

Plangi / Pelangi - Reservefärbe- und Musterungs-verfahren, bei dem Stoffteile vor der Anwendung von Farbstoffen durch Abbinden mit färbebestän-digen Fasern ausgespart werden. Die Muster be-stehen üblicherweise aus kleinen Kreisen

Prada - in Südostasien gebräuchlicher Begriff für die Goldklebetechnik oder den Auftrag von Gold-blatt oder Goldstaub auf eine Stoffoberfläche

Sarong - zu einem schlauchförmigen Rock zusam-mengenähtes Tuch, das stets einen *kepala*-Teil auf-weist. In westlichen Quellen wird der Begriff „sarong" oft wahllos für die flachen wie auch die schlauchförmigen Tücher verwendet (Schreibweise auch „sarung")

Sawat - Muster aus der *larangan*-Gruppe, das sich vermutlich aus dem Palmettenmuster der Kunst des Nahen Ostens und Südasiens entwickelte. Auf Java interpretiert man es als symbolische Darstel-lung von *Garuda*

Selendang (sprich: slendang) - schmales, rechtecki-ges Schultertuch oder Schal, das Frauen diagonal über der Schulter trugen

Sembagi-Stoffe - bedruckte Stoffe von der Koro-mandel-Küste, die noch im 19. Jahrhundert in großer Zahl nach Sumatra exportiert wurden

Semen - stilisierte Darstellung einer heiligen Land-schaft

Sidangan - rautenförmiges Feld bei den Kemben für verheiratete Frauen. Sichtbares Symbol ihres Status als Ehefrau

Soga - in der javanischen Batik verwendeter brau-ner Farbstoff, der durch eine Kombination von Rinde und Holz verschiedener Bäume gewonnen wird. Eine wichtige Zutat ist die Rinde des Soga-Baumes, peltrophorum ferrigineum. Je nach Her-stellungsregion erscheint *soga* in verschiedenen Schattierungen

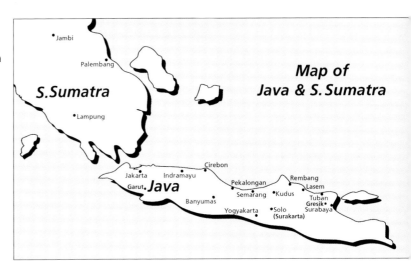

Tambal - beliebtes Motiv bei der Musterung zent-raljavanischer Stoffe. Gruppe von Batikmustern, die wie ein Patchworkstoff erscheinen

Tjanting - *canting*

Tok wi - wörtlich: „Sitz der Götter". Häufig mit Batiktechnik verziertes Altartuch bei Chinesen am Hausaltar

Tritik - Reservefärbe- und Musterungsverfahren, bei dem der Stoff vor der Anwendung von Farb-stoffen genäht, gerafft und fest zusammengezo-gen wird, so dass die Farbe nicht in die ausgespar-ten Stoffteile eindringen kann. Nach dem Färben werden die Nähte entfernt, und es erscheint das Muster

Tulis - „Schreiben"; Batiktechnik, bei der das Auf-tragen des Wachses mit dem *canting* vorgenom-men wird

Tumpal - sich gegenüberliegende Reihen lang ge-zogener Dreiecke im *kepala* eines *sarongs*

Wayang - „Puppen" aus Leder oder Holz, die beim Erzählen von Geschichten aus den Epen Ramayana und Mahabharata und anderen Erzählungen im Schattentheater eingesetzt werden. Als Batik-motive verwendet

A young Indo-Chinese girl, probably
a njahi or concubine, 1897,
photo by Hung Wan Foon, Medan, Sumatra

Glossary

badan - "body" of a sarong; it forms the largest part of a sarong. The other part is known as the "head" (see: *kepala*)

bang - red colour which is the unifying feature of almost all batiks produced on North Java

bang-bangan - fabrics dyed with just the red colour

bangun tulak - black and white *kemben*. Used as a protective cloth in most vulnerable moments of life such as pregnancy or sickness

batik - resist-dyeing process in wich a substance such as hot wax or rice paste is applied on the surface of fabric as a resist to dyes to form undyed areas of pattern. The resist is removed by boiling, melting or scraping after dyeing

batik cap - batik cloth in which the patterns are stamped on with a special metal stamp

batik kaligrafi - fabrics produced for Sumatra, decorated with quotes from the Koran and invocations of Allah in Arabic script

batik tulis - batik cloth in which the patterns are drawn with the canting tool (see *tulis*)

buta - tear-drop motif in India, which features prominently in the decoration of Kashmiri shawls (see *lar*)

buyr - uniform decorative design on *kemben*; suitable for unmarried women

canting - Javanese name for a small batik tool consisting of a wooden or bamboo handle with a copper reservoir from which one ore more spouts permits the controlled application of the molten wax to the surface of the cloth

cap - Javanese term for a metal stamp, usually constructed of strips of sheet copper, used in the batik process to apply molten wax to the surface of the cloth. A cap contains an entire design unit

celana - batik trousers, often worn by Chinese and European residents on Java

cherki - card game of southern Chinese origin, popular among the Straits Chinese communities of Singapore, Malacca and Penang, as well as of Indonesia, especially before the war. It was a popular pastime among the womenfolk, and was played in the home: not only during a normal day, but also at festive occasions such as birthday and new year celebrations and sometimes even at funerals

ciptoning - *wayang* design on batik textiles

dodot - long hip cloth, about four times the length of a *sarong*, formerly worn by members of the royalty, the aristocracy and court dancers, and draped around the body in a variety of ways

garuda - mythical bird. The mount of the God Vishnu in Hindu mythology

iket kepala - head cloth for men used for formal occasions, tied in a variety of ways to form a turban

indigo - *nilo*. Blue dye derived from plants of the Indigofera and Marsdenia species, by producing an active precipitate from the reaction of the leaves with an alkaline solution

kain - generic term commonly used for flat, rectangular cloths

kain bang-biru - batiks of North Java featuring blue and red - the most common colour combination of laseman fabrics

kain kelengan - fabrics of North Java dyed with only dark blue or black; they are worn as mourning dresses

kain kembangan - "flowered cloths". *Kemben* in which the technique of batik has been combined with other types of resist dyeing such as *plangi* (tie-dye) and *tritik* (stitch-dyeing)

kain laseman - batiks produced at Lasem in Chinese workshops. The design indicates the influence of Indian chintz textiles as well as Chinese iconography

kain panjang - "long cloth" or hip cloth, approximately 250 cm long, 105-110 cm wide, worn on more formal occasions. The unsewn cloth is wrapped around the hips by both men and women, with the last section usually arranged in a series of pleats in front, which fan out when the wearer walks

kain sprei - bed cover

kawung - famous old motif formed from parallel rows of circles. There are many variations

kebaya - loose garment with wide sleeves made of white calico, originally worn by women of mixed Portuguese or Chinese descent

kemben - breast or chest cloth for women

kepala - "head" of a *sarong*, consisting of an upright standing rectangle with color and pattern which are different from the "body" (see *badan*)

kraton - Javanese palace, in Yogyakarta and in Surakarta in Central Java

kris - dagger. Exemplifies the male aspect of the universe. In the official court dress of Central Java, a batik skirt and kris/dagger are always worn together

kudhung - rectangular cloth, slightly wider than a selendang, worn as a head and shoulder covering by Muslim women

lar - design representing a single wing of the *Garuda* bird. It was destined for persons of lower rank at Javanese courts (see *buta*)

larangan - group of "forbidden" designs. Their use was restricted to the sultan and high court officials since the end of 18th century

laseman - *kain laseman*

latar putih - "white background". Technique, in which coloured designs appear on a light, undyed background. One of the most difficult batik designs represented in *kain laseman*

mengkudu - red dye obtained from the roots of the mengkudu shrub (morinda citrifolia). The source of the bright red color found on pasisir batik

mui li (chines.) - door curtain, often decorated with batik and hung over the door of the bridal chamber during a Peranakan or Chinese wedding. They can also be hung above other doors in the house during special ceremonies or on occasions such as the Chinese New Year

nilo - *indigo*

nitik - Javanese batik design translating the indian *patola* design. The execution of this design in wax requires the use of a specially constructed canting

pagi sore - morning-late afternoon. A diagonally bisected format with a mostly light half (morning) and a mostly dark half (late afternoon) for, respectively, daytime and evening wear

parang - famous diagonal "knife" motif, consisting of a series of alternating light and dark bands in contrasting colors, bounded by undulating or scalloped edges. The design was traditionally reserved for royalty

parang rusak - "broken dagger". Motif composed of continuous, wavy bands which run in diagonal rows across the whole surface of the cloth

pasisir - North coast of Java (used to refer to any coastal region)

patola - trade textiles from India, recognised as the most luxurious of all Indian fabrics. Silk cloth decorated with the technique of double ikat, *patola* designs do not feature continuous lines but are built of tiny, square, drop-like units (see *nitik*)

peranakan - Chinese residents of the Indonesian and Malay archipelago whose families have lived in the region for several generations (as opposed to the so-called "totoks", Chinese newly arrived from the mainland)

plangi / pelangi - resist-dyeing and patterning process in which areas of cloth are reserved from dye by being bound off with dye-resistant fibres before dyestuffs are applied. Patterns are usually built up from small circles

prada - term widely used in Southeast Asia for gold leaf gluework, the application of gold leaf or gold dust to the surface of the cloth

sarong - cloth sewn to form a tubular skirt. It always includes a *kepala* section. In Western sources, the term *"sarong"* is often used indiscriminately for both the flat and tubular cloths (also used as "sarung")

sawat - design from the larangan group, probably evolved from the palmette design appearing in the art of the Near East and South Asia. On Java it is interpreted as a symbolic representation of *Garuda*

selendang (pronounced: slendang) - narrow, rectangular cloth, worn diagonally across a woman´s shoulder

sembagi fabrics - printed cloths from the Coromandel Coast, which used to be exported to Sumatra in large quantities even in the 19th century

semen - stylised rendition of the sacred landscape

sidangan - diamond-like field on *kemben* worn by married women. Visual symbol of their wedded status

soga - brown dye used in Javanese batik, derived from a combination of bark and wood from several trees. A major ingredient is the bark of the soga tree, peltrophorum ferrigineum. Depending on the region in which it is made, soga occurs in various shades

tambal - favourite motif decorating Central Javanese fabrics. Assemblage of batik designs which imitate patchwork cloth

tjanting - *canting*

tok wi (chines.) - seat for the ancestors. Cloth often decorated with batik to cover the ancestral altar in a Chinese family home

tritik - resist-dyeing and patterning process in which the cloth is stitched, gathered, and tucked tightly before dyestuffs are applied so that dye cannot penetrate the reserved areas. Once the color has been applied, the stitching is removed, showing the patterns

tulis - "writing". A batik technique where wax is applied with the *canting* tool.

tumpal - elongated triangles placed in rows facing each other in the *kepala* of a *sarong*

wayang - puppets, made of leather or wood, used in telling stories from the Ramayana, Mahabharata epics and other stories. Used as a batik motif

Danksagung

Dieser Katalog ist eine Art Gesellenstück zu meinem 65. Geburtstag. Er ist nicht das Werk von vier Monaten. Diese Zeit bezieht sich allein auf die Realisierung des Buchprojektes als solches. In Wirklichkeit ist er das Ergebnis von 30 Jahren Sammeltätigkeit, während derer mich zahlreiche Persönlichkeiten begleitet haben und die damit ebenso Anteil an diesem Buch haben: als Kritiker und als Schmeichler; als Bremser und als Motor; als Ideengeber und Ideen-Ausführer; als Lehrer und als Lernende; als Vorreiter und als Nachahmer, als lebendes Vorbild oder als Mahnung und Erinnerung an Tod und Vergänglichkeit. Allen diesen Begleitern bin ich sehr verbunden. Und allen, die ihren Namen hier erwarten und nicht lesen, bin ich es ebenso. Die Zahl 65 setzte mir die Grenze.

Daly Adjas (†) · Inta Amolina · Amri Yahya (†)
Pak Ansaruddin · Ardiyanto Pranata
Bagong Kusudiardjo (†) · Brunhilde Berke (†)
Joachim Blank · Thierry Bogaert · Brian Brake (†)
Donald Breyer · Jaques Coenye
Vipula Dharmawardene · Alit Djajasoebrata
Munir Djody · Nian S. Djoemena · Noel Dyrenforth
Diane L. Fagan Affleck · Sergio Feldbauer (†)
August Flick (†) · Gianto C.P. · Annegret Haake
Leo Haks · Sri Sultan Hamengku Buwono X
Alfons Haryadi · Adrian Idris · Jonathan Hope
Mary Hunt Kahlenberg · Fiona Kerlogue
John Kreifeldt · Eiko Adnan Kusuma · Peter Lee
Chan Chia Lin · Johann-Borwin Lüth
Brigitte Majlis-Khan · Yamin Makawaru (†)
Ici Mardisi (†) · Robyn Maxwell · Karl Mertes
Didier Millet · Elizabeth Moeljohardjo (†)
Emmi und Paula Möller (†) · Thomas Murray
Pak Nasrun (†) · Ibu Nusyati (†) · Erik Oey
Bambang Oetoro (†) · Irene Romeo (†)
Kristine Scherer · Carl-Wolfgang Schümann (†)
Rüdiger Siebert · Hans-Wilhelm Siegel (†)
Pak Soemihardjo (†) · T.T. Soerjanto · Beatrijs Sterk
Nyoman Sukajahadi · Jacek Szelegejd
Chua Thean Teng (†) · Christiane Thalemann
Irmgard Timmermann · Rita Trefois
Harmen C. Veldhuisen · Tuan Waloejo (†)
Peter Wenger · Brigitte Willach
Shinobu Yoshimoto · Noor Azlina Yunus
Renate v. Zitzewitz (†)

Mein Dank geht zunächst an all diejenigen, die am Zustandekommen und an der Realisierung des Kataloges wesentlich beigetragen haben: Gisela Büscher für die Betreuung der Batiken; der Fotograf Fulvio Zanettini für perfekte Aufnahmen der Textilien; Hans van der Kamp für die Überlassung der historischen Fotos aus seiner großen Sammlung; Jan Konietzko und Team für das gelungene und überzeugende Layout; Oliver Drüg für sorgfältigen Druck. Gute Übersetzerinnen werden oft nicht erwähnt und sind doch so wichtig. Ich danke Susanne Mattern und Maria Schlatter herzlich für Ihren Einsatz. Fiona Kerlogue danke ich für ihre Kooperation sowie guten Ratschläge am Telefon und per email. Sabine Philipp danke ich sehr gerne für ihre große und professionelle Hilfe bei der Koordination, bei der Redaktion und dem Lektorat. Sie war darüber hinaus mein unermüdlicher Motor mit Blick auf den Kalender und initiierte dankenswerter Weise das Interview, das noch manche Fragen offen lässt aber dem Leser einige aufschlussreiche Antworten bietet.

Ganz besonders bedanke ich mich bei den Freunden und bei meiner Frau Karin, die mir bei der Realisierung der Ausstellung und des Kataloges mit Rat und Tat zur Seite standen: Jede(r) hat seinen/ihren wesentlichen Teil zum Gelingen beigetragen.

Mein besonderer Dank geht jedoch an die beiden Autorinnen, die professionell und kompetent ihre so lesenswerten Beiträge für diesen Katalog verfasst und mir zur Verfügung gestellt haben. Isa Fleischmann-Heck hat ein eigentlich trockenes historisches Thema „Batik von 1906 bis 1920" so anschaulich und spannend dargestellt, dass man sich auf die Fortsetzung „Batik von 1920 bis 1973" schon freuen darf. Für die Batik-Forschung hat sie damit einen ganz wesentlichen Beitrag geleistet. Maria Wronska-Friend, mit der mich eine über 20-jährige Batik-Freundschaft verbindet, hat ihr großes Wissen auf diesem Gebiet kurz, kompetent und übersichtlich ausgebreitet. Von Australien aus, fernab von Köln, trug sie neben dem Fachartikel auch die Abbildungsunterschriften zu den Batiken meiner Sammlung bei.

Der Museums-Direktorin Brigitte Tietzel danke ich für ihr schmeichelhaftes Vorwort. Und besonders für die Möglichkeit, meine Sammlung in den schönen Räumen des Deutschen Textilmuseums einem interessierten Publikum in der Samt und Seiden-Stadt Krefeld zeigen zu dürfen. Mein Dank wendet sich damit auch an das Team des Museums mit Isa Fleischmann-Heck als Kuratorin und den Restauratorinnen.

Zuletzt, aber nicht weniger herzlich danke ich meinem Freund Donald Harper für die ehrlichen und informativen Antworten in dem gemeinsamen Interview. Ohne seinen unermüdlichen Entdeckergeist und seine Risikobereitschaft hätte ich diese Sammlung historischer Batiken niemals zu dem machen können, woran wir uns heute erfreuen.

Mit diesem Katalog-Buch möchte ich auch den unbekannten Kunst-Handwerkerinnen meine Referenz erweisen für ihren Beitrag zu der großen Geschichte der Batik.

Ich bereue es nicht, mich als Sammler für die Batik entschieden zu haben und allmählich sehen auch jene, die früher gelächelt und einen Umweg um Java gemacht haben, die ganze Vielfalt, Schönheit und die Einzigartigkeit dieser Kunstwerke.

Rudolf G. Smend   Köln, 21. August 2006

Acknowledgements

I consider this catalogue as a kind of journeyman's piece on my 65th birthday. It is not the work of four months, which was merely the time needed to put the book project as such into effect. In reality, it is the result of 30 years of collecting, during which time I have been associated with numerous people who also have a share in the creation of this book: as critic or flatterer; as hindrance or driving force; as inspiration or doer; as teacher or student; as pioneer or imitator; as living role model or as reminder of death and transience.

I feel a strong connection to all those who have accompanied me on my journey, including those who expect to find their name here and do not.

I have had to set a limit at 65.

Daly Adjas (†) · Inta Amolina · Amri Yahya (†)
Pak Ansaruddin · Ardiyanto Pranata
Bagong Kusudiardjo (†) · Brunhilde Berke (†)
Joachim Blank · Thierry Bogaert · Brian Brake (†)
Donald Breyer · Jaques Coenye
Vipula Dharmawardene · Alit Djajasoebrata
Munir Djody · Nian S. Djoemena · Noel Dyrenforth
Diane L. Fagan Affleck · Sergio Feldbauer (†)
August Flick (†) · Gianto C.P. · Annegret Haake
Leo Haks · Sri Sultan Hamengku Buwono X
Alfons Haryadi · Adrian Idris · Jonathan Hope
Mary Hunt Kahlenberg · Fiona Kerlogue
John Kreifeldt · Eiko Adnan Kusuma · Peter Lee
Chan Chia Lin · Johann-Borwin Lüth
Brigitte Majlis-Khan · Yamin Makawaru (†)
Ici Mardisi (†) · Robyn Maxwell · Karl Mertes
Didier Millet · Elizabeth Moeljohardjo (†)
Emmi und Paula Möller (†) · Thomas Murray
Pak Nasrun (†) · Ibu Nusyati (†) · Erik Oey
Bambang Oetoro (†) · Irene Romeo (†)
Kristine Scherer · Carl-Wolfgang Schümann (†)
Rüdiger Siebert · Hans-Wilhelm Siegel (†)
Pak Soemihardjo (†) · T.T. Soerjanto · Beatrijs Sterk
Nyoman Sukajahadi · Jacek Szelegejd
Chua Thean Teng (†) · Christiane Thalemann
Irmgard Timmermann · Rita Trefois
Harmen C. Veldhuisen · Tuan Waloejo (†)
Peter Wenger · Brigitte Willach
Shinobu Yoshimoto · Noor Azlina Yunus
Renate v. Zitzewitz (†)

First of all, I am grateful to everyone who has made a significant contribution to the realisation and production of this catalogue: Gisela Büscher for supervising the batiks; the photographer Fulvio Zanettini for the perfect photo shoots of the textiles; Hans van der Kamp for loaning the historic photographs from his great collection; Jan Konietzko and his team for the excellent and effective layout; Oliver Drüg for the meticulous printing. Good translators are very important yet often do not receive the recognition they deserve. I thank Susanne Mattern and Maria Schlatter very much for their dedicated efforts.

I would also like to thank Fiona Kerlogue for her cooperation and good advice given by phone and email. I am very happy to thank Sabine Philipp for her great and professional help during the project coordination and editorial production. She was furthermore an untiring driving force, always keeping an eye on the calendar. Thankfully, she also organised the interview, which although it may still leave many questions open, nevertheless provides a number of revealing insights.

I am especially indebted to my friends and my wife Karin, who helped me with both advice and practical support during the implementation of the exhibition and the catalogue. Each one of them has made a significant contribution to their success.

My particular thanks go to the two authors, who wrote professional, expert and very readable contributions to this catalogue and allowed me to use them. Isa Fleischmann-Heck has managed to present a rather dry historic subject, "Batik from 1906 until 1920", in such an interesting and stimulating manner that we look forward to the second instalment, "Batik from 1920 until 1973". She has made a vital contribution to the study of batik. Maria Wronska-Friend, whom I have known as a fellow batik enthusiast and friend for over 20 years, has presented her enormous knowledge in this field succinctly, expertly and clearly. Writing in Australia, far from Cologne, she also provided the captions for the batiks from my collection, in addition to her specialist article.

I am grateful to the museum director, Brigitte Tietzel, for her flattering preface, and above all for the opportunity to be able to show my collection in the beautiful galleries of the German Textile Museum to an interested public in the "velvet and silk town" of Krefeld. My thanks are therefore also directed at the museum team, including the curator, Isa Fleischmann-Heck, and the restorers.

Last, but by no means least, I extend my heartfelt thanks to my friend Donald Harper for his honest and informative answers given during our joint interview. Without his untiring pioneering spirit and his willingness to take risks, I would never have been able to develop this collection of historic batiks into that which we can enjoy today.

I have tried to pay tribute to the anonymous craftswomen and to express my appreciation of their enormous contribution in the batik tradition.

I don´t regret having decided in favour of batik and gradually even those people, who in the past turned up their noses and shunned Java, are able to recognize the full diversity, beauty and exceptionality of these artefacts.

Rudolf G. Smend   Cologne, August 21. 2006

Empfohlene Literatur ab Erscheinungsjahr 1999
Select Bibliography since 1999

Achjadi, Judi (ed.): Batik. Spirit of Indonesia. Editions Didier Millet. Jakarta / Singapore 1999

Batik Jawa Hokokai, Catalogue of the exhibition, Pusat Kebudayaan Jepang, Jakarta 2000

Breguet, Georges: La fibre des ancêtres. Trésors textiles d'Indonésie de la collection Georges Breguet. Infolio éditions, Genève 2006

Coenye, Jacques: Batik 2003. Kunst in Beweging, Art in Motion. Gent 2003.

Doellah, H. Santosa: Batik. The Impact of Time and Environment. Danar Hadi, Solo 2002

Duggan, Geneviève: The Chinese batiks of Java. In: Hout van, Itie C. (ed.): Batik - Drawn in Wax. 200 Years of Batik Art from Indonesia in the Tropenmuseum Collection. Royal Tropical Institute, Amsterdam 2001, pp. 90 - 105.

Dyrenforth, Noel: Batik: Modern Concepts and Techniques. B.T. Batsford, London 2003.

___, Batik: Neue Techniken, moderne Konzepte. Haupt Verlag, Bern 2004.

Elliott, Inger McCabe: Batik. Fabled Cloth of Java. 2nd edn, Periplus Editions, Singapore 2004

Fleischmann-Heck, Isa / Tietzel, Brigitte: Weltwunder. Textilien der Sammlung Henkel Düsseldorf, Catalogue of the exhibition, Deutsches Textilmuseum Krefeld 2005. Krefeld 2005

Friend, Maria Wronska: Javanese batik for European artists. Experiments at the Koloniaal Laboratorium in Haarlem. In: Hout van, Itie C. (ed.): Batik - Drawn in Wax. 200 Years of Batik Art from Indonesia in the Tropenmuseum Collection. Royal Tropical Institute, Amsterdam 2001, pp. 106 - 123

___, Batik and Kris: Duality of the Javanese Kosmos. In: Conference Proceedings of the World Batik Conference, Massachusetts College of Art, Boston 2005. Boston 2005

___, Painted with Wax. Batik on Java and in Poland. Catalogue of the Exhibition "Painted with Wax - Javanese and Polish Batik featuring Rudolf G. Smend collection, Köln", The State Ethnographical Museum in Warzaw 2006. Warszawa 2006
Gittinger, Mattiebelle: Textiles for this world and beyond. Treasures from Insular Southeast Asia. Scala, London 2005

Haks, Leo / Wachlin, Steven: Indonesia. 500 EarlyPostcards. Editions Didier Millet, Singapore 2004

Hitchcock, M. / Nuryanti, Wiendu (eds.): Building on Batik - The Globalization of A Craft Community. Proceedings of the Dunja Batik Conference, Aldershot / Ashgate. Yogyakarta 1997

Hout van, Itie C. (ed.): Batik - Drawn in Wax. 200 Years of Batik Art from Indonesia in the Tropenmuseum Collection. Royal Tropical Institute, Amsterdam 2001

Kahlenberg, Mary Hunt / Tuttle, Richard: Indonesian Textiles. Tai Gallery / Textile Arts, Santa Fe, NM 2004

Kerlogue, Fiona G.: The Batik of Madura. In: Hout van, Itie C. (ed.): Batik - Drawn in Wax. 200 Years of Batik Art from Indonesia in the Tropenmuseum Collection. Royal Tropical Institute, Amsterdam 2001, pp. 66 - 77

___, Flowers, Fruits and Fragrance: The batiks of Jambi. In: Hout van, Itie C. (ed.): Batik - Drawn in Wax. 200 Years of Batik Art from Indonesia in the Tropenmuseum Collection. Royal Tropical Institute, Amsterdam 2001, pp. 78 - 89

___, Islamic Talismans: The calligraphy batiks. In: Hout van, Itie C. (ed.): Batik - Drawn in Wax. 200 Years of Batik Art from Indonesia in the Tropenmuseum Collection. Royal Tropical Institute, Amsterdam 2001, pp. 124 - 135

___, The book of Batik. Featuring selections from the Rudolf G. Smend Collection. Editions Didier Millet, Singapore 2004

___, Batik. Design, Style & History. Thames & Hudson, London / New York 2004

___, Batik Ontwerp, stijl en geschiedenis. Uitgeverij Atrium, Rijswijk 2005

Knight-Achjadi, Judi / Damais, Asmoro: Butterflies and phoenixes. Chinese inspirations in Indonesian Textile Arts. Mitra Museum Indonesia, Jakarta 2005

Kusuma, Eiko (ed.): The Islands of Cotton. Textiles in Indonesia. The Eiko Kusuma Collection. The Fukuoka Art Museum, Fukuoka 2003

Legêne, Susan / Waaldijk, Berteke: Reverse images - patterns of absence. Batik and the representation of colonialism in the Netherlands. In: Hout van, Itie C. (ed.): Batik - Drawn in Wax. 200 Years of Batik Art from Indonesia in the Tropenmuseum Collection. Royal Tropical Institute, Amsterdam 2001, pp. 34 - 65

Masao, Izawa (ed.): Superfine Selections of International Batik combined Exhibition in Saitama. Catalogue of the exhibition, The Museum of Modern Art, Saitama, 2002. Saitama 2002

Maxwell, Robyn J.: Sari to Sarong. Five Hundred Years of Indian and Indonesian Textile Exchange. Catalogue of the exhibition, National Gallery of Australia 2003. National Gallery of Australia, Canberra 2003

___, Textiles of Southeast Asia. Tradition, Trade and Transformation. 2nd edn, Periplus Editions, Singapore 2003.

Sacred Threads. Ceremonial Textiles of Southeast Asia. Textile Friends of Singapore. Catalogue of the exhibition, Asians Civilisations Museum Singapore 2001/2002. Singapore 2001

Smend, Rudolf G. (ed.): Batik I. Batiken von Fürstenhöfen und Sultanspalästen aus Java und Sumatra. Sammlung Rudolf G. Smend. Galerie Smend, Köln 2000

___, Batik - From the Courts of Java and Sumatra, Rudolf G. Smend collection. 2nd edn, Periplus Editions, Singapore 2004

Soerjanto, Toetti: Batik - The impact of time and environment. In: The Pekalongan Batik Museum - Bridging Time and People. Paper of the conference Pekalongan 2005. Pekalongan 2005

Tirta, Iwan: Creating New Directions for Traditional Indonesian Batik. In: The Pekalongan Batik Museum - Bridging Time and People. Paper of the conference Pekalongan 2005. Pekalongan 2005

Wenger, Peter: Batik Retrospektive. Catalogue of the exhibition, Galerie Smend, Köln 2005/2006. Galerie Smend, Köln 2005

___, Indigo-SogaBrown/Mengkudu Red. In: Conference Proceedings of the World Batik Conference, Massachusetts College of Art, Boston 2005. Boston 2005

Bis Erscheinungsjahr 1999 / until 1999:

Smend, Rudolf G. (ed.): Batik. Batiken von Fürstenhöfen und Sultanspalästen aus Java und Sumatra. Sammlung Rudolf G. Smend. Galerie Smend, Köln 2000

Weitere Literatur siehe Literaturverzeichnis in / further reading see: Kerlogue, Fiona, Batik. Design, Style and History. Thames & Hudson, London / New York 2004

Detail No. 2, S./p. 63

Kurzbiografien/Contributors

Isa Fleischmann-Heck studierte Kunstgeschichte, christliche Archäologie und Germanistik an den Universitäten von Aachen, Freiburg i. Br. und Bern. Nach ihrer Promotion in Kunstgeschichte arbeitete sie 1997/1998 als Volontärin am Museum für Angewandte Kunst in Köln. Von 1999 bis 2001 war sie im Gutenberg-Museum in Mainz als wissenschaftliche Mitarbeiterin beschäftigt. Seit 2002 ist Isa Fleischmann-Heck stellvertretende Museumsleiterin im Deutschen Textilmuseum Krefeld. Ihre Arbeitsschwerpunkte sind Druckstoffe, die Textilkunst des 19. und 20. Jahrhunderts sowie Ost- und Südostasiatische Textilien.
E-Mail: fleischmann-heck@krefeld.de

Isa Fleischmann-Heck studied history of art, archeology and German literature at the Universities of Aachen, Freiburg i. Br. and Bern. She worked at the Museum of Applied Arts in Cologne and at the Gutenberg-Museum in Mainz. Since 2002 Isa Fleischmann-Heck has been Curator at the German Textile Museum in Krefeld, specializing in printed textiles, Art Nouveau and modern textiles, and East-Asian textiles. She has an MA from the University of Freiburg i. Br. and a PhD in history of art from the University of Bern.
E-mail: fleischmann-heck@krefeld.de

Dr. Maria Wronska-Friend ist „Adjunct Senior Lecturer" an der Universität James Cook in Australien. Die polnisch-stämmige Anthropologin und Museumskuratorin ist seit über zwanzig Jahren von den Kostümen und der Textilkunst Südostasiens fasziniert. Ihren Doktortitel erhielt sie an der polnischen Akademie der Wissenschaften in Warschau für ihre Arbeit über den Einfluss javanischer Batik auf die europäische ornamentale Kunst um die Wende des 19./20. Jahrhunderts. Sie führte weitreichende Feldforschung in Indonesien, Papua-Neuguinea und in der australischen Einwanderergemeinde der Hmong durch. Die Ergebnisse ihrer Forschungsarbeiten wurden in zahlreichen Publikationen sowie in mehr als zehn größeren Ausstellungen in Australien und Europa präsentiert.
E-Mail: m.friend@cairns.qld.gov.au

Dr Maria Wronska-Friend, Adjunct Senior Lecturer at James Cook University, Australia, is a Polish-born anthropologist and museum curator who, for more than twenty years, has been fascinated by South-East Asian costumes and textile art. She received her PhD from the Polish Academy of Sciences in Warsaw for investigating the influence of Javanese batik on European decorative arts at the turn of 19/20th centuries. She has conducted extensive fieldwork in Indonesia, Papua New Guinea and among the Australian community of Hmong migrants and has presented the results of her research in numerous publications and through more than ten major exhibitions in Australia and Europe.
E-mail: m.friend@cairns.qld.gov.au

Der Amerikaner Donald J. Harper sammelt traditionelle Textilien, insbesondere indonesische Batik. Seit 1975 lebt er in Südostasien. Er spielte eine wichtige Rolle bei der Akquisition vieler der schönsten Stücke in der Sammlung Rudolf G. Smend, die in diesem Buch gezeigt wird. Zudem vermittelte er viele Textilien, die sich heute in verschiedenen wichtigen Museumssammlungen befinden, z. B. im Nationalmuseum Singapur, im Los Angeles County Museum of Art, im Fowler Museum der University of California Los Angeles, im Rautenstrauch-Joest-Museum für Völkerkunde in Köln und im Deutschen Textilmuseum Krefeld. Neben seiner Tätigkeit als Sammler schöner alter Stücke arbeitet er gegenwärtig eng mit mehreren zeitgenössischen Textilkunsthandwerkern zusammen, um die Entwicklung neuer Textilien von hoher Qualität in Indonesien, Brunei und Malaysia zu fördern und so einen Beitrag zur Bewahrung alter Techniken und Traditionen südostasiatischer Textilkunst zu leisten.
E-Mail: batikman@gmail.com

Donald J. Harper is an American collector of traditional textiles, particularly Indonesian batik. He has lived in Southeast Asia since 1975. He played a significant role in acquiring many of the finest pieces which are part of the Rudolf G. Smend collection of batik featured in this book. In addition, he has sourced many textiles which are now part of a number of important museum collections, such as the National Museum of Singapore, the Los Angeles County Museum of Art, The Fowler Museum at UCLA, the Rautenstrauch-Joest-Museum of Ethnology in Cologne and the Textile Museum Krefeld. Besides collecting fine old pieces, he is currently working closely with a number of contemporary textile artisans to further develop the creation of new, high quality textiles in Indonesia, Brunei, and Malaysia in order to help preserve some of the ancient techniques and traditions of Southeast Asian textile art.
E-mail: batikman@gmail.com

Rudolf G. Smend, Autor, Herausgeber, Sammler und Galeriebesitzer, kam zum ersten Mal im Jahr 1972 im indonesischen Yogyakarta mit Batik in Berührung. Seitdem hat er sein Leben der Batik gewidmet. Er wurde oft als maßgeblicher Redner zu Konferenzen und Veranstaltungen zum Thema Textil geladen (Yogyakarta, Jambi, Washington DC, Gent, Berlin und Boston). Er ist der Eigentümer der Galerie Smend in Köln, die Werke internationaler Textilkünstler ausstellt und vor kurzem ihr 33-jähriges Bestehen feierte. Smend war als Herausgeber und Verleger zahlreicher Bücher zu Batik und Seidenmalerei tätig, z. B. „Seidenmalerei Handbuch I -VI" und „Batiken von Fürstenhöfen und Sultanspalästen aus Java und Sumatra: Sammlung Rudolf G. Smend". 2005 war er der europäische Berater der World Batik Conference in Boston, die als Begleitveranstaltung zu einer Ausstellung seiner Sammlung in Lowell, MA am American Textile History Museum stattfand.
E-Mail: rudolf@smend.de

Rudolf G. Smend, author, editor, lecturer, collector and gallery owner; he was first introduced to batik in 1972 at Yogyakarta, Indonesia. From that time on, his life has been dedicated to batik. He has often been invited as an authoritative speaker to textile conferences and events (Yogyakarta, Jambi, Washington DC, Ghent, Berlin and Boston). He is the owner of the Smend Gallery in Köln, Germany which exhibits the work of international textile artists and recently celebrated its 33rd anniversary. Smend has edited and published numerous books on batik and silk painting including "Seidenmalerei Hanndbuch I-VI" and "Batiks from the Courts of Java and Sumatra: the Rudolf G. Smend collection". He was the European Advisor to the World Batik Conference in Boston 2005, accompanying the exhibition of his collection in Lowell, MA at the American Textile History Museum.
E-mail: rudolf@smend.de

Impressum / Imprint

Fotonachweis/Photo Credits

K. Cephas: S./p. 60
Charls & Co Photographen: S./p. 45
A.S. Cohan: S./p. 58-59
Deutsches Textilmuseum Krefeld: S./p. 10, 14
Hung Wan Foon, Medan, Sumatra, S./p. 166
Photos by Dieter Gasse: S./p. 10-25
Leo Haks, Amsterdam: front jacket
Museum Kratonan, Yogyakarta: S./p. 5
Tan Tjie Lan: S./p. 54, 164
Sie Sie Lin: S./p. 62
„Textile Kunst und Industrie": S./p. 17, 20, 25
W.B. Woodbury: S./p. 40
Photographer unknown: front jacket, S./p. 6, 9-10, 19, 27,
27, 33, 36-37, 38, 43, 49, 50, 56, 156, 178-179, back jacket
Collection R. G. Smend: S./p. 130, 145

Disclaimer:

Herausgeber/Editor:
Rudolf G. Smend, Köln

Übersetzung/Translation:
Susanne Mattern, Karben
Maria Schlatter, London

Redaktion/Editoring:
Sabine Philipp, Bonn

Layout:
Jan Konietzko, Köln
www.ci-werk.de

DTP:
Ulrike Strunden, Köln

Fotograf/Photographer:
Fulvio Zanettini, www.zanettini.net

Druck/Print:
UDK UbiaDruckKöln
www.ubiadruck.de

Verlag/Publisher:
Galerie Smend, Köln
www.smend.de
© 2006 Verlag der Galerie Smend, Köln,
Printed in Germany

Historische Fotos/Historical Photos:
Leihgeber/Lender:
Hans van der Kamp, Antiquariaat Minerva
Den Haag, vdkamp-o1@planet.nl

Bildbearbeitung/Scan:
Jan Overduin, Rotterdam, look@coverall.nu

Ausstellungsorte/Exhibition locations:

Deutsches Textilmuseum Krefeld
Andreasmarkt 8, 47809 Krefeld-Linn
fon +49(0)2151-94 69 45-0
fax +49(0)2151-94 69 45-55
textilmuseum@krefeld.de
www.krefeld.de/textilmuseum
24.9.2006 - 30.12.2006
Konzeption/Conception:
Isa Fleischmann-Heck
Brigitte Tietzel

Galerie Smend, Mainzer Strasse 31, 50678 Köln
fon +49(0)221-31 20 47
fax +49(0)221-932 07 18
smend@smend.de
www.smend.de
22.9.2006 - 28.10.2006

Veröffentlicht in Verbindung mit der Ausstellung
„Javanische Batiken" der Sammlung Rudolf G. Smend
im Deutschen Textilmuseum Krefeld
vom 24. September bis 30. Dezember 2006.

Published in conjunction with the exhibition
"Javanese batiks". The Rudolf G. Smend Collection
held at the Deutsches Textilmuseum Krefeld
from September 24th to December 30th 2006.

ISBN -10:   3-926779-65-9
ISBN -13: 978-3-926779-65-6

Detail No. 24, S./p. 83

Women batiking, ca. 1890